The Clydebank Blitz

I. M.

Books are to be

© I. M. M. MacPhail, 1974

ISBN 0 9537736 2 0

Published by
West Dunbartonshire Libraries & Museums

Reprinted
1991, 1995, 2000

Printed by
Cordfall Ltd
Glasgow

PREFACE

Since March, 1941, when Clydebank bore the brunt of the German air raids on Clydeside, stories of what happened have appeared from time to time. During the period of the war, reasons of security prevented any detailed reference to location or the extent of the bombing, although press interviews added some colour to the impersonal statements from the Ministry of Home Security. At the beginning of 1972, the official files on the raids in the Scottish Record Office in Edinburgh and the Public Record Office in London became available for research, and it was then decided by Clydebank Town Council that the time had come for a full and objective account of what happened. It has not been an easy task as there are many gaps in the records, and it would be impossible at this date to give a complete picture of events. I have been fortunate, however, in being able to supplement the official records by interviews with a number of those who were present in Clydebank during and immediately after the raids.

It is a pleasure for me to acknowledge the assistance, willingly given, by so many people, in particular, Mr. J. A. G. Hastings of Galashiels (former Depute Town Clerk of Clydebank), Mr. Kenneth MacLeod of Killin (formerly Depute Chief Constable of Dunbartonshire), Dr. Alexander Jamieson of Skegness, Mr. R. A. Nixon, Town Clerk, Clydebank, and Councillor Robert Calder of Clydebank.

I. M. M. MacPhail

German Aerial Photograph of Clydebank

CONTENTS

PART ONE—BEFORE THE RAIDS

PAGE

Pre-War Civil Defence 1
Air Raid Precautions 3
Shelters 5
Fire Services 6
A.R.P. Emergency Committee 9
Blitzkrieg 11
Night Raids 12

PART TWO—THE RAIDS

The Alert 15
German Raiders 16
First Bombs 17
Clydebank Ablaze 19
Fire-fighting 21
Bombs and Mines 23
Major Incidents 25
Casualty Services 27
The Final Year Medicals 29
Police 31
Control Centre 35
Friday's Respite 37
The Second Raid 40
Rescue Parties 42
Ack-Ack and Night Fighters 44

Dogs, Cats and Canaries 47
Evacuation 48
Rest Centres 50
Private Billets 54
Post-Raid Problems 56
Bomb Disposal 58
Water Supply 59
Industrial Production 63
Burying the Dead 64
Casualty Figures 66
Curiosities 68
Conclusion 69

APPENDICES

A. List of Fatal Casualties 71
B. Notable Night Attacks on U.K. Cities, November, 1940-May, 1941 94
C. Luftwaffe Attack on Glasgow and Clydeside, March 13-14, 1941 95
D. Luftwaffe Attack on Glasgow and Clydeside, March 14-15, 1941 96
E. Effect of Raids of March 13-15, 1941 on Industrial Concerns 98
F. List of Bombs Dropped on Clydebank, March 13-15 and May 5-7, 1941 100
G. Roll of Honour 107
H. Extracts from School Log of Dumbarton Academy, Session 1940-41 108

ILLUSTRATIONS

	Facing Page
German Aerial Photograph of Clydebank	V
Destruction at Singer's factory	1
Devastation at "The Holy City"	16
A.R.P. Officials, Clydebank, 1939 - 45	17
Dalmuir West Tramway Terminus	32
Leaving Home, Radnor Street, Clydebank	33
The Morning After	48
Emergency Drinking Supplies	49
Hosiery Mill Duntocher	64
Dumbarton Road, Old Kilpatrick	65
Funeral of Unclaimed Victims	70
Blitz Memorial, Dalnottar Cemetery	71
Heroes of the Clydebank Blitz	108

Illustrations reproduced by kind permission of *The Glasgow Herald and The Evening Times*

Destruction at Singer's factory

PART ONE

BEFORE THE RAIDS

Pre-War Civil Defence

The first attempts by the British Government to prepare the civilian population for defence against aerial bombing were made in 1935. For well over two years some local authorities, including the Town Council of Clydebank, refused to co-operate in the proposed voluntary arrangements. In the early 1930's, hopes had been entertained that the League of Nations might bring about disarmament all round; but a Disarmament Conference at Geneva collapsed in 1934 when Germany, just after Adolf Hitler had come to power, withdrew from the Conference and the League of Nations. In March of the following year, Hitler introduced military conscription, and the Italian leader, Mussolini, began to make threatening noises about Italy's claims to Abyssinia. Re-armament was now regarded by the British Government as a necessity but at first no great urgency was shown. Stanley Baldwin, who succeeded Ramsay MacDonald as Prime Minister in 1935, put forward proposals for re-armament, which met with criticism from nearly all sections of the Labour Party and the Trade Union movement, particularly from the pacifist minority, including the leader of the Parliamentary Labour Party, the veteran George Lansbury.

In Clydebank Town Council, the Labour Party had achieved a majority at the election in November, 1934; and when they met in September, 1935 to consider the Scottish Office Circular 3026, setting forth certain suggested precautions for Local Authorities in preparation against possible enemy air raids, the Labour majority took up the standpoint of those on the left wing of the national party and decided by 10 votes to 5 not to co-operate with other authorities in the country in a voluntary scheme as recommended in the Circular from the Scottish Office. Councillor John Green, himself an old soldier, moved for co-operation with the other county authorities and was seconded by Police Judge Peters, while the amendment, which carried, was proposed by Councillor Davidson and seconded by Councillor Downie.

In 1936, re-armament in Britain was speeded up in view of the increasingly menacing attitude of Nazi Germany and Fascist Italy. The mood in the Labour Party itself changed somewhat at the time of the Italian invasion of Abyssinia in 1935, when the League of

1

Nations was considering the imposition of sanctions against Italy as an aggressor state. At the Labour Party Conference at Brighton in October, 1935 Scottish Trade Union and Labour Party circles still tended to favour opposition to re-armament; and George Lansbury, true to his pacifist ideals, appealed to the members of the Conference for support in his last speech as party leader, quoting Jesus Christ, 'Those who take the sword shall perish by the sword'. He was scathingly attacked, however, by Ernest Bevin, who accused him of 'trailing his conscience round from body to body, asking to be told what to do with it.'

Clydebank Town Council contained many members who, though not adhering to the pacifist position of Lansbury, felt strongly that co-operation with the Government over air-raid precautions was condoning not only the Government's defence measures but also its foreign policy. David Kirkwood, who then represented Clydebank and Dumbarton Burghs in Parliament, had declared amid applause, at a pre-election meeting in Clydebank in October, 1935: 'I am all out for peace in the real sense and would not send a Clydebank boy to war upon any consideration. No war for me under any circumstances.' Opposition to war itself was widespread and natural in 1935 but it may be said that opposition to defence against enemy attack was unrealistic. The Clydebank Councillors, however, like many others felt that the Government's defence measures were no substitute for a foreign policy which was based on collective security instead of being one of appeasement. It was not surprising, therefore, that the Town Council in March, 1936 (just two days after Hitler's Nazi troops had re-occupied the Rhineland) declined to send representatives to a conference on air-raid precautions, the motion to adhere to their former decision being carried by 13 votes to 5. Gradually, however, recalcitrant councils throughout the country were conforming to the Government's directive and in January, 1937, the only Scottish local authorities refusing to co-operate were Clydebank, Wick and Tranent. Clydebank's decision in 1937 not to co-operate was made despite an earnest appeal made once more by Bailie John Green. By the end of 1937, at last, the Government decided on compulsory measures and carried through the Air Raid Precautions Act in December of that year. Without further ado, Clydebank Town Council agreed to implement the Act and in the spring of 1938 set about making preparations against air raids.

What was the effect of the long protracted delay in implementing the Government's recommendations? According to one senior official of the period, it seemed as if the Town Council had decided to make up for lost time and lost opportunities by pushing on with the necessary measures with a sense of urgency, and by the time that war came, probably little, if anything, had been lost. Indeed, the earlier air raid precautions had tended to be improvisations and in one sense Clydebank had profited by the experience of other authorities. The burgh officials in Clydebank felt that in the immediate pre-war period there was a tremendous pressure of work involved in setting up the machinery envisaged in the A.R.P. Act of 1937; but it seems, at any rate, as if Clydebank was at least as prepared in that respect as any comparable burgh in Scotland.

Air Raid Precautions

The announcement that Britain was at war with Germany was made by the Prime Minister, Neville Chamberlain, from 10 Downing Street in a broadcast on the morning of Sunday, September 3rd, 1939, and his brief speech was interrupted by the wailing of an air raid warning siren. This had actually been caused by the unannounced approach of a civilian passenger plane from France but it symbolised the jittery state of nerves in which most people were in the first days of the war that nearly everyone listening to the broadcast immediately concluded that German bombers had reached London. In Clydebank, already on the previous Friday, September 1st, school-children, carrying gas-masks and identity cards, had been evacuated to reception areas such as Helensburgh. Windows of public buildings were sand-bagged, those of houses and shops were blacked out so that no light shone through, and A.R.P. Wardens patrolled the streets at night to check on any careless householder. Civilians and service-men went about carrying gas-masks, and young mothers were faced with the worry and anxiety of how to protect their babies, for whom special equipment against gas attacks was later provided in the form of a 'Mickey Mouse' mask. Poison gas was the terrible fear that gnawed at people's minds and although, as we know now, it was never used, both sides prepared carefully for what was officially described as chemical warfare. Nor did the expected air raids come, at least for the first year, the period of the 'phoney war'. Air raid sirens did sound in Clydebank and district on at least forty occasions before March, 1941 (the siren signalling the onset of heavy bombing on March 13th was actually the first of that year apart from practice sirens); but mostly the warnings were for single planes on reconnaissance, some of them taking photographs which were later to be used in connection with the air raids. In time schoolchildren and other evacuees began to trickle back, although many remained away for the duration of the war. Normal schooling was resumed but the senior secondary pupils travelled daily to Dumbarton Academy, where some Clydebank children were to be found in the sixth form as late as 1949.

Air raid precautions (or A.R.P. as they came to be called) involved the formation of various services and the establishment of control centres and district posts—A.R.P. Wardens' Posts, First Aid Posts, Ambulance Teams, Rescue Squads, Decontamination Squads, and an Auxiliary Fire Service. In addition, provision was made for the construction of bomb-proof shelters, the issue of gas-masks, the control of lighting during hours of darkness, and many other and diverse precautions. The various A.R.P. services underwent regular training and were gradually provided with suitable premises and equipment, although as late as March, 1941, as we shall see, the arrangements were still open to criticism. One of the difficulties encountered in Clydebank was that of recruitment to the voluntary services as so much overtime was worked in the local shipyards and factories engaged in war production that even men and women keen to join in one or other of the Civil Defence Services could not guarantee to be present when required.

By March, 1941, however, there were 462 A.R.P. Wardens in Clydebank, of whom 50 were full-time paid personnel. All Wardens were obliged to turn out on an air raid warning and in addition had regular tours of duty. The A.R.P. Wardens of the burgh were divided into five groups, each covering a district of the town similar to the election wards. For example, 'D' Group had its Control Centre at the present Clydebank High School, then called Janetta Street School, as the building had not been completed. The Wardens' Posts in March, 1941, were three in number—one at a hut on the site of the present Pinetrees Hotel on the Boulevard, one on the site of the present Parkhall Branch Library, and one in Boquhanran Church Hall where, as there was no telephone, messages were brought over from the Control Centre in Janetta Street School.

In addition to the A.R.P. Wardens, who were best known to the public before the raids, patrolling the streets and visiting houses to check on the black-outs of windows, etc., there were other services, which were to be even more important in the event of a serious raid. The Casualty Services, under the Medical Officer of Health, Dr. Hunter, were based on two First Aid Posts, one in Elgin Street

School and one in Boquhanran School, and four First Aid Party and Ambulance Depots. They comprised 16 First Aid Parties, of which eight were full-time, and had at their disposal, in addition to 23 ambulances, 18 cars available for sitting cases. There were also eight Rescue Parties, of which four were full-time paid personnel, mostly composed of workers in the building trades, capable of dealing with the arduous work of clearing away debris after bomb damage in the search for survivors. Decontamination Squads were also organised in readiness for the poison gas attacks, expected to take the form of sprays that would leave the ground saturated. In addition, there were about 90 part-time messenger boys of about sixteen to eighteen years of age, drawn mainly from youth organisations such as the Boys' Brigade and Boy Scouts, who were to perform wonderful feats of daring and heroism during the air raids when telephonic communications were disrupted. The police force, supplemented by war-time special constables, were able, in addition to their normal duties, to play a co-ordinating role and some of the police officers were specially trained as A.R.P. officers.

Shelters

The provision of shelters was increasingly recognised as a matter of urgency following the German raids on London in the winter of 1940-41. There the underground 'Tube' provided ready-made shelters for thousands, some people sleeping on platforms and corridors nightly for months on end. In Clydebank, as elsewhere in the United Kingdom, people with gardens were supplied with shelters, which were half-buried in the ground. These were called Anderson shelters after Sir John Anderson, a civil servant who later became a member of the Government. As it was stipulated that only those who paid National Health Insurance contributions or had an income of less than £5 a week could receive these shelters free, there were a number of families without them. At first, the Anderson shelters, which consisted of 14 corrugated steel sheets, with a corrugated steel hood, curved for greater strength, and sunk about two feet in the ground, were large enough to accommodate as many as six persons, but later slightly smaller shelters were provided. These, it was proved by tests, could withstand without damage the effects of a 500 lb high-explosive bomb going off 50 feet away and give protection against blast from a similar explosion 30 feet or more away. They were to save many lives in Clydebank and elsewhere but at first there were some people who would not or could not have them erected. In the summer of 1940, powers were given to the local authorities to erect them for such householders who were genuinely incapable of doing so themselves and take the shelters away from those who were considered capable of doing so but still refused. As a result, nearly all people entitled to an Anderson shelter had one in the garden, perhaps among the cabbages or the rosebeds or even in the middle of the lawn. The Anderson shelter could be made quite cosy and comfortable but there were complaints about dampness, as might be expected, and at a special meeting of Clydebank Town Council just before the 'Blitz' in March, 1941, it was reported that all such cases of dampness had been dealt with except for 30 newly-erected shelters in North Kilbowie. Even these, however, were to prove their worth in the 'Blitz'.

In the case of tenement buildings, there were two types of shelters provided. In the Dumbarton Road and Glasgow Road area of Clydebank, a number of the closes were strutted with steel-tube scaffolding as a protection for the people living in the close, who were expected to leave their own homes in the event of an air raid and sit inside the close at the ground floor level. To guard against the effect of blast being tunnelled up the close from a bomb exploding nearby, baffle walls were erected at the edge of the pavement and in the back court opposite the entry to the close. As the streets on moonless nights were very dark indeed, baffle walls could offer difficulties to the ordinary pedestrian, although most people carried small torches in the time of the 'black-out'. In other streets, surface shelters, built at first of brick and concrete and later of ferro-concrete, were erected in open spaces, e.g. in the back courts. These shelters had no windows and, as they were dark and sometimes damp, they were not regarded with much favour by residents of tenements. The provision of chemical closets became a necessity but did not add to the attractiveness of the shelters. Both types of shelters, strutted closes and surface shelters, were to be found invaluable in the 'Blitz'.

Fire Services

Before the Second World War there was no National Fire Service. This came into being only in August, 1941, mainly as a result of the experiences of the heavy air raids in 1940-41. The Burgh of Clydebank at the beginning of the war had, like other comparable large burghs, its own Fire Brigade, with a strength of 14 in March, 1941. In addition, there had been developed in the heavily populated areas before the war, in anticipation of heavy air raids, an Auxiliary Fire Service. The A.F.S., as it came to be known, contained full-time paid personnel, and as the work involved was of necessity dangerous and arduous, it tended to attract a high proportion of young recruits, a number of whom left in the first year of the war to join the fighting services. In June, 1940, the Government announced that men between the ages of thirty and fifty might volunteer for the A.F.S. in place of military service and this measure helped to maintain the A.F.S. at a reasonable level. In the Battle of Britain of 1940 and the winter 'Blitz' on London which followed, the firemen there were more exposed to enemy attack than most of the soldiers in the Army. The A.F.S. were not equipped with self-propelled fire engines like the regular Fire Brigades but with trailer pumps, the main reason being to provide as many pumps as possible as quickly as possible and at a reasonable cost. In addition they could be man-handled over debris, where the self-propelled machines could not proceed. For towing vehicles, the A.F.S. were at first authorised to buy second-hand high-powered cars and lorries, but as these proved at times unsatisfactory and unreliable, they were later supplemented by specially designed 2-ton vans.

Fire-fighting however was not left only to the Fire Brigade and the A.F.S. As far back as 1937, the Home Office had advocated for the use of the average householder a pump with a foot support, which for that reason came to be known as the stirrup-pump. It was later fitted with a dual-purpose nozzle, the spray of which could be used on an incendiary bomb and the jet on any fire which developed. These were at first issued to A.R.P. Wardens' Posts and to fire authorities, who were expected to train volunteers for supplementary fire-parties. The supply of stirrup-pumps in the first years of the war continued to be small and the cost of provision high, so that widespread criticism greeted the Home Secretary who in a broadcast urged 'every householder to get a stirrup-pump and to learn to use it'.

Lack of fire-fighting appliances was one weakness in Civil Defence which the Government began to appreciate belatedly. Another was the problem of unoccupied premises—offices, factories, shops, schools, churches, many of them with large spreads of roofs which could form catchment areas for incendiary bombs. After the holocaust in London on December 29-30, 1940, the War Cabinet decided on the principle of compulsion for part-time civil defence, which meant in effect fire-watching for people at the places where they were

employed.   Clydebank Town Council, like other councils, was to
check the arrangements made for fire-watching in business premises
and public buildings and also help to organise street fire-watching
and fire-fighting parties through the A.R.P. Wardens.   One problem
in Clydebank, as a result of this Fire Prevention (Business Premises)
Order of January, 1941, was the lack of sufficient men available for
fire-watching in the employment of the Halls and Baths Sub-Committee, the shortage being due to the large number of employees
already in Civil Defence.   It was agreed by the Town Council to ask
for volunteers from other members (including female employees) of
the Council's staff to take up fire-watching duties, which commenced
on February 15th, 1941.

Clydebank Town Council's other duty of organising fire-watching
parties on a voluntary basis was in process of being carried out just
at the time of the 'Blitz' in March, 1941.   In order to rouse public
interest in fire prevention, a meeting was held in the Town Hall on
Tuesday, February 25th, 1941, when a disappointingly small
audience heard appeals from Police-Judge Green, fresh from a visit
to London, advising all citizens to go to the lectures on fire-prevention
in the Town Hall and to a demonstration at the Cleansing Department yard on how to extinguish an incendiary bomb.   Councillor
King said that Thomas Johnston when A.R.P. Regional Controller
for Scotland (he had just become Secretary of State for Scotland a
week or so before) had expressed his disappointment with the
position in Clydebank and had hoped there would be an improve-
ment.   Bailie Peters paid tribute to the people of John Knox Street
for the enthusiastic way in which they had responded to the fire
prevention appeal.   Some criticism of the authorities dragging their
feet came from an A.R.P. Warden present at the meeting, Richard
Scott, who contradicted Provost David Low's statement about the
lack of preparedness and co-operation.   He claimed that in the
Second Ward there was hardly a close not organised for fire-fighting.
He had himself submitted a list of a thousand names from Kilbowie
Road to the Canal Bridge and he blamed the departments concerned
for the lack of proper organisation.   Another member of the public,
Mr. Clelland, pointed out that many people worked late and could
not attend fire prevention demonstrations and he criticised some
house factors who were unwilling to clear their lofts.   In the case of
MacAlpine's property in Kilbowie, Councillor King said that they
now discovered that there was only one hatch giving access to the
roof for every third close, and as the roofs were of tarmacadam,

there was great danger if incendiaries fell. (Three weeks later, his fears were realised in the devastating fire which destroyed the 'Holy City', as MacAlpine's property was called.) Another rate-payer, who raised the question of the shortage of sandbags and stirrup-pumps, was assured by the Provost that the A.R.P. Emergency Committee was doing all in its power to ensure an adequate supply.

As it happened, time was running out for the authorities and for the townspeople. At a special meeting of the Town Council in March, 1941, just before the 'Blitz', dissatisfaction was expressed about the state of affairs so far as fire-watching parties were concerned. Provost Low reported that 3,133 persons had enrolled for fire prevention duties but they were not all registered, so that they or their relatives could not claim compensation in case of injury. But Councillor Mrs. Stewart maintained that many people had given in their names to Wardens for fire-fighting duties and never heard any more about it. As a tail-piece to this account of Clydebank's difficulties in organising fire-fighting parties, it might be mentioned that on March 13th, 1941, there were only two stirrup-pumps in the whole area covered by the A.R.P. 'D' Group; and a meeting of householders in Chestnut Drive in the house of Robert Elder, himself a Warden, to consider ways and means of purchasing stirrup-pumps, buckets, etc., was interrupted by sirens sounding to signal a German air raid. Finally, it must be pointed out here that it is extremely doubtful if, particularly in the tenement areas, the existence of properly equipped fire-fighting parties would have made much difference on the nights of March 13-14 and 14-15, 1941.

A.R.P. Emergency Committee

The overall responsibility for Air Raid Precautions in Clydebank was vested in a sub-committee of the Town Council, the A.R.P. Emergency Sub-Committee, which in 1940-41 consisted of eleven members—Provost David Low (convener); Bailies Waterson and Green, Police Judges Brown and Wood, Councillors Fleming, MacLaren, King, Paul and Boyle. The executive control was exercised by the Town Clerk, Henry Kelly, A.R.P. Controller for the burgh, and his Depute, James A. G. Hastings, with the assistance and co-operation of all the heads of departments—the Burgh Surveyor, the Medical Officer of Health, the Sanitary Inspector, the Firemaster, etc. Much of their time was devoted to implementing the instructions contained in the innumerable circulars emanating from Government departments. The Ministry of Home Security, responsible for defence of the civilian population, had an office in Glasgow, from which issued several hundred circulars in 1940 and 1941, dealing with the various aspects of air raid precautions, e.g. the contingency of a breakdown in telephone communications; the reporting of parachute mines dropped in the Clyde; the rendezvous points for reinforcements during air raids (in Clydebank, three Wardens' Posts, one a mile west of the Kilbowie Road—Boulevard intersection, a second on Glasgow Road at the Hamilton Street junction, and a third at the junction of Dumbarton Road and Mount Blow Road); the control of mobile canteens after a raid; gas vans and fixed gas chambers for gas training; ventilation conditions in public shelters; leather boots for Rescue Parties; methods of dealing with incendiary bombs; greyhound race meetings, etc., etc. The Department of Health in Edinburgh was no less assiduous in their distribution of information and the Emergency Committee's files of circulars grew thicker and thicker as the war proceeded.

The energies of the civil servants were not confined to issuing circulars. Any proposals involving expenditure by Local Authorities on Civil Defence had to be approved by the appropriate Department or Ministry, and too often the burgh officials found their proposals changed or rejected simply because they differed in some degree from the official instructions contained in the original circular. One example related to the Control Centre for the burgh, which the local officials and councillors felt should be situated on the periphery of the town and not at or near the Municipal Buildings, because of their proximity to John Brown's shipyard, inevitably a primary target in any German air raid. They were overruled, however, by the civil service mandarins, and the basement of the Public Library was finally chosen as the Control Centre. This decision was based partly on the civil servants' preference for a central as opposed to a peripheral location and partly on the fact that the dimensions of the rooms in the Library basement coincided closely with those laid down in the official specifications in the circular on Control Centres. As it happened, the Library (as well as the Town Clerk's Office) received a direct hit in the night of the first raid and the Control Centre became a shambles, fortunately without fatal casualties. Too often, the Clydebank officials and councillors felt themselves frustrated by the attitude of the civil servants, whom some wag christened 'inverted Micawbers, sitting in their office chairs, waiting for something to turn down'. One last aspect of this frustration may be mentioned. When Fergus Roberts, Town Clerk of the neighbouring burgh of Dumbarton, visited the Clydebank Town Clerk, Henry Kelly, on the morning of March 14th, 1941, after the first raid, he found him amidst the debris resulting from the explosion of a bomb in the Municipal Buildings. Kelly was naturally very much overwrought after the night's experience but managed to pick up for Roberts to examine a file of letters relating to expenditure on fire-hose, which the Ministry had been unwilling to approve.

Blitzkrieg

Long before the outbreak of hostilities in September, 1939, military theorists had tended to be unanimous in their forecast of the next war as likely to be won quickly and decisively by a sudden, intensive aerial bombardment of the civilian population in the great cities, paralysing the enemy's industry, transport and communications. This theory of lightning war had been propounded at great length by an Italian general, Douhet, and an American, Billy Mitchell; but in the late 1930's it was linked especially with the Germans, who had started, after Adolf Hitler's accession to power, to build up their armed forces, especially their air force or Luftwaffe. The German word *Blitzkrieg* means 'lightning war'; and it was this name which was to become used universally in the first months of the Second World War.

The Germans themselves started war on September 1st, 1939, at dawn by launching a *Blitzkrieg* on Poland, bombing the Polish airfields and destroying most of the Polish air force on the ground, hammering railway centres, and sending their armies streaming into Poland. In April, 1940, in another version of *Blitzkrieg*, German paratroops were dropped at important strategic points in Norway; airfields and ports were seized with the help of a Norwegian 'fifth column' and before long the Germans had overrun Norway. A month later, Holland was conquered by the use of German paratroops as in Norway but also by a pitiless bombardment of Rotterdam in which over 30,000 were killed. It was as a result of this raid on Rotterdam that Churchill, who had just replaced Neville Chamberlain as Prime Minister, sanctioned the bombardment of industrial targets in Germany, which meant also the bombing of the civilian population, and British bombers raided the Ruhr. Until the bombing of Rotterdam, air raids on both sides had been confined officially to military objectives; and indeed, so quiet had been German operations on the Western front that the period of the first winter of the war, 1939-40, was described as the 'phoney war'. After Holland,

Belgium fell to the Nazi forces, and then France, the British troops being evacuated from Dunkirk but leaving behind them thousands to languish in German prisoner-of-war camps.

The summer of 1941 saw the fierce contest for supremacy of the air between the Royal Air Force and the Luftwaffe, which is known today as the Battle of Britain. Victory in this was essential for the Luftwaffe if a German invasion was to be undertaken but it eluded them, thanks to British fighter squadrons and a Scotsman's invention, radar. During the Battle of Britain, aerial warfare was conducted at first in daylight but latterly, in October, the Luftwaffe chief, Hermann Goering, resorted to night raids. London suffered grievously during the ensuing winter; on 82 out of 85 consecutive nights German bombers raided the capital. It was then that the word 'Blitz' passed into popular usage in the sense of a heavy aerial bombardment rather than in the original sense of a lightning war. To many people, the word adequately described their idea of the air raid: it was a German word and, like lightning, it came from the sky and it killed people. From its first application to the German raids on London, 'Blitz' came to be used of the heavy raids on other cities and towns, including Clydebank.

Night Raids

The winter of 1940-41 is for ever associated in the minds of the British people with hardships—the black-out, rationing, fire-watching, air raid shelters, bombs; and the wail of the siren can still send a chill down the spine of many a person who survived the 'Blitz'. The German Luftwaffe's transition from daylight to night air raids was undertaken primarily because, although they were not so accurate, they were less likely to lead to the loss of bombers and crews. The main objectives for the Luftwaffe, as for the R.A.F. in Germany, were industrial targets, such as aircraft factories, engineering works, docks, shipyards, oil tanks, railways, canals; but inevitably the civilian population nearby came under attack. Throughout the winter of 1940-41, German air-crews were briefed to bomb industrial targets such as those mentioned above, and the crews in their reports claimed hits on or near such targets. Yet there is little doubt that these raids were intended to undermine the morale of the civilian population, for example in the use in built-up areas of parachute mines, which could not be aimed but floated down to explode on impact, creating a tremendous lateral blast which shattered houses. In this policy of destroying the morale of those on the home front by aerial bombardment, events were to prove the Germans wrong. 'We can take it,' claimed the 'blitzed' Londoners, as also did the 'blitzed' people of Hull, Coventry, Portsmouth, Southampton, Bristol and Clydebank.

The night raids of 1940-41 by the German Luftwaffe had nevertheless a considerable degree of success from their point of view. By the use of clever devices such as radio navigation beams, they were able to bomb selected targets even on dark nights. The normal routine was for a small pathfinder force of aircraft, equipped with sophisticated instruments, to arrive at the target area, release flares to light up the scene, drop high-explosive and incendiary bombs in order to start fires, which were then 'markers' for subsequent waves of bombers. London remained the chief target for the Luftwaffe throughout the winter but one of the worst raids of the period occurred on the night of November 14-15, 1940, when about 450 German aircraft, led by a pathfinder unit, raided the midland city of Coventry, which then had a population of nearly 200,000. It was a night of bright moonlight and German aircraft streaming in over the Wash, over the Isle of Wight and over Brighton had no difficulty in finding their objectives. In less than an hour, the centre of the city was an inferno: telephone lines were destroyed, gas and water mains damaged, railway lines blocked and in the course of the night over 550 people were killed. Despite several hits on 21 important factories, 12 of them concerned with the aircraft industry, within a few weeks production in most works was back to normal but it took months, if not years, before the centre of Coventry was restored to life again.

British radio counter-measures proved more and more effective as the winter went on. They at first involved jamming the signals emitted from Luftwaffe stations and later 'bending the beam', to direct the enemy aircraft away from their target. But they did not prevent the Germans devastating the city of London on December 29th, 1940, when there resulted an even worse fire than that of 1666 and enormous damage was wrought at the dock warehouses along the Thames. The Londoners' worst raid of all came as late as May 10th, 1941, when the House of Commons was destroyed along with other notable buildings.

Before then, the Luftwaffe had made raids regularly in suitable weather on the large industrial cities of the United Kingdom. (A table showing the heaviest raids of 1940-41 is provided in Appendix B.) The bad weather of January and February caused a falling-off in large-scale raids but in the spring the attacks were renewed and increased in intensity throughout March and April until the middle of May. Hitler had by this time long since abandoned the plan of an invasion of Britain and was contemplating an 'about-turn' —the invasion of Russia; and the German Luftwaffe's exertions over Britain were intended to mask Hitler's preparation for a Russian campaign. In addition to the constant 'Blitz' on London, German attacks were delivered in the west and particularly on ports— Plymouth, Liverpool, Birkenhead, Bristol, Avonmouth, Glasgow and Clydebank.

British defences were being strengthened all this time. Radio counter-measures thought out by the 'boffins' or 'back-room boys', as they were called, sometimes had German aircraft navigators so bewildered that crews landed in south-west England thinking they were in France. Anti-aircraft ('Ack-Ack') batteries, searchlight posts, balloon barrages were increased in numbers and improved. Decoy-fires, known by the code name of 'Starfish', were prepared in the vicinity of large cities and likely targets, to be lit when a German raid commenced in order to induce the follow-up forces to drop their bombs away from their real targets. In addition, lights were arranged at 'Starfish' sites near ports to simulate those at docks, where of necessity unloading and loading were often carried on at night-time. On the north bank of the Clyde such a decoy system was installed on the hills above Clydebank on Cochno Estate and similarly above Dumbarton at Auchenreoch and Kipperoch; and in the raids of March and May, 1941, a great number of bombs found their way to the decoy sites which might otherwise have fallen on Clydebank and Dumbarton. Nightfighters were not very successful until the spring of 1941. Liaison with anti-aircraft batteries was naturally very important: in practice, A-A fire reached 12,000 feet and the nightfighters operated above this altitude. The Bristol Blenheim, originally a medium bomber, was converted to a nightfighter, with five ·303 Browning machine-guns and equipped with the new A.I. (aircraft interception) radar; and the Blenheims (and Beaufighters later on) proved most effective in the last German raids of 1941. And yet, with all these counter-measures and much more thorough preparations for civil defence, some towns, like Clydebank, received their worst raids just before the Germans turned their attention to the East.

PART TWO

THE RAIDS

The Alert

In mid-March, 1941, the West of Scotland enjoyed a spell of glorious spring weather. The rooks were building their nests in the tall trees at Mount Blow, carts of blaes were being delivered at the local tennis courts, and with the advent of double summer-time allotment-holders were using the extra daylight after working hours to make a beginning with the spring work. The five local cinemas regularly attracted full houses in those days before television. On Thursday, March 13th, Shirley Temple and Jack Oakie could be seen in 'Young People' at the La Scala and the Regal, Dalmuir; Jean Hersholt, starred as the 'pocket Ginger Rogers', was on view at the Pavilion; at the Bank Cinema there was a film about horse-racing in America called 'Maryland'; and at the Palace, in addition to the film, 'Daughter of the Tong,' Carrol Levis was on show with his 'Discoveries'. Many people were to spend the first hours of the 'Blitz' in these cinemas. It was the normal procedure when an air raid alert was sounded for the manager to inform the audience, some of whom had of necessity to leave, while the majority usually remained in their seats; and as there had been no raid in Clydebank since before the New Year, most people on March 13th tended to stay put at first. When it became evident, however, that bombs were dropping all over Clydebank, the programmes came to an end but many stayed on in the cinemas, gathering under the balcony for safety.

During the war, listening to the 9 o'clock news on the B.B.C. Home Service was almost a ritual in many households. On Thursday, March 13th, 1941, the 9 o'clock news had just started when the wail of the air-raid sirens was heard sounding the alert. Some listeners in Clydebank at first felt sorry for London again suffering an attack from the German Luftwaffe but then it became only too clear that the sirens were sounding in Clydebank and all over the West of Scotland. John R. Third, later principal teacher of English in Clydebank High School, was walking down Kilbowie Road just after the dismissal of his class in the old High School at 9 o'clock when the sirens sounded. The evening school pupils whose classes went on until 9.30 p.m. were marshalled into the school playground shelters, (sometimes an alert lasted only for ten minutes or so) and James

Shankie, later depute rector in Clydebank High School, used to recount years afterwards his feelings of helplessness when a German flare seemed to be dropping towards the school, illuminating the whole area. The sirens put all the Civil Defence services on the alert. Wardens off duty donned their tin hats or helmets, slung their gas-masks over their shoulders and hurried off to their posts. Casualty services were actually engaged in their usual Thursday evening practice just before the sirens sounded so that there was a full turn-out of personnel in a very short time. Town Councillors had been attending committee meetings—Fire and Lighting, Housing, and Cleansing (the latter had under consideration a letter from the Second Ward Committee protesting about the closure of a public lavatory in Whitecrook Lane). But the committee meetings ended well before the alert and some of the Councillors were already in the Control Centre in the basement beneath the Public Library along with Henry Kelly, the Town Clerk and Civil Defence Controller for Clydebank, and other officials who had gathered there following a preliminary warning. This had been sent about 7.30 p.m. from the Civil Defence District Control 'War Room' in Glasgow, when it had been discovered that a German radio-navigational beam was directed to Clydeside.

German Raiders

It was a beautiful moonlight night when the German raiders swept upon Clydeside. A 'bomber's moon' rode high in the sky, just as on the night in November, 1940, when Coventry was raided; and rivers and railways showed clearly to aircraft 12,000 feet above. According to the secret and confidential report from the Luftwaffe Headquarters next day, conditions were favourable to the attacking aircraft both in regard to weather and visibility: not only could the target areas be clearly identified but, it was claimed, the crews could distinguish the craters made by the bombs. In the report it was stated that 'from 22.30 to 6.47 hours' (21.30 to 5.47 by British time) '236 bombers attacked along the length of the River Clyde with about 272 tons of high explosive bombs and 1650 incendiary containers'. The bombers were mostly Heinkel 111's and Junkers 88's and among the units employed was K.Gr.100, the famous pathfinder unit which had first operated in such a role in the raid on Coventry on November 14th, 1940.

The German aircraft made their way to the Clyde by three different routes: one started from Beauvais in Northern France, some of the

Devastation at "The Holy City"

CLYDEBANK CIVIL DEFENCE, WARDENS SERVICE—SENIOR OFFICERS, 1939 - 1945

Front Row—Staff Off. W. McFarlane, Div. Wards. J. Longden (F), Mrs. J. Hyslop (E), R. Turner (A), Controller C.D., H. Kelly, Chief Warden A. J. V. Cameron, Training Officer Inspector A. Macdonald, Div. Wards. C. MacKenzie (B), W. Laurie (D), W. Bowie (D).

Second Row—Sen. Ward. A. Little, Head Wards. E. Connell, H. Brown, Div. Wards. R. Baird (A), T. H. Overend (C), Head Ward. T. Rae, Sen. Ward. S. McLintock, Head Ward. J. Menzies.

Back Row—Sen. Wards. D. Rendall, P. Wallis, W. Ross, R. Caldwell, D. McMillan, E. Brash, A. McKellar, J. Johnston.

units returning to Amsterdam, another from bases in Holland and North Germany, and a third, used by aircraft later on in the raid, from Stavanger in Norway and Aalborg in Denmark. The main force, which came from Holland and North Germany, approached Britain near Hull and crossed the coast line at places between the Tees and the Tweed. People living in Edinburgh could hear the drone of these planes just as people in Aberdeen did in the small hours of the morning. The Clyde river and estuary were clearly discernible features under the light of the full moon but many aircraft which came in from the east and north-east first arrived over Loch Lomond, whose silvery expanse of water, dotted with islands, made it easily identifiable, and then flew southwards down the Vale of Leven to the Clyde. The German objectives were not confined to Clydebank but included Glasgow: indeed, German official reports on the raids of March 13th-14th and 14th-15th refer to 'the raids on Glasgow', Clydebank being regarded by them, with some justification, as part of the Glasgow conurbation.

British radio counter-measures intended to interfere with the German navigation devices by jamming the signals or 'bending the beams' operated only in the districts of the large English cities, London, Liverpool, Manchester and Birmingham, so that the Luftwaffe had a clear run to the west of Scotland. It was, however, not only Clydeside which the Germans raided on the night of March 13th-14th, 1941. 65 aircraft bombed Liverpool and Birkenhead before midnight and dropped 58 tons of high-explosive bombs and 122 incendiary containers, as a follow-up of the previous night's massive raid when 316 German planes dropped 303 tons of high-explosive bombs and 1,782 incendiary containers, while at Hull, between 10 p.m. and 2.25 a.m. 78 bombers dropped 39 tons of high-explosive bombs and 125 incendiary containers. The raids on Liverpool-Birkenhead and Hull finished comparatively early and seem to have been intended as diversions; but the raid on Merseyside, the second on successive nights, fitted into the pattern of German bombing of industrial centres in 1940-41, as Clydebank was to find out the following night.

First Bombs

Tuesdays and Thursdays were the practice evenings for ambulance teams in Clydebank in 1941, and they had actually been rehearsing on the evening of March 13th for an inter-depot competition. Hugh Campbell, one of the ambulance drivers at the Dalmuir depot, was shortly after 9 p.m. putting the ambulances back into the lean-to shelters at Singer's Ground when an incendiary bomb landed at the entrance to the shelter. After kicking the incendiary out of the way, he phoned the Control Centre just when a bomb exploded some-where in the vicinity. Almost immediately, a message came from the Control Centre to proceed to Beardmore's Diesel Works at Dalmuir. On the way there, the ambulance team saw another bomb fall on the public house at the corner of Beardmore Street and Dumbarton Road. Later, when his ambulance was returning with casualties aboard, a bomb exploded near-by, killing two of the injured men. Campbell, badly shaken, clambered out of the wrecked ambulance and made his way to the depot about three-quarters of a mile away. There he obtained another ambulance, with which he returned to pick up the survivors and brought them to hospital. For this and other actions performed by him during and after the raids, when for four days and nights he had no sleep, Hugh Campbell was awarded the O.B.E.

By 9.30 p.m. the first wave of German bombers had arrived and high explosive bombs and incendiaries were falling in the lower parts of the town. The bombs were at first small ones, 50 kilo bombs, and the intention of the raiders was first to drive people, including fire-fighters, to seek shelter and then to pour down incendiaries to start marker fires for the bombers following later. According to some eye-witnesses, Beardmore's Diesel Works at Dalmuir was the first place or one of the first to be hit, but a police officer, now retired, maintains that the first bomb landed on the south side of Second Avenue opposite the junction with Albert Road. According to others, the first major incident was in Whitecrook Street, when fatal casual-ties occurred at No. 57 and No. 59. These bombs may well, of course, have landed at or about the same time as those in Dalmuir. In the same part of the town, beside the Forth and Clyde Canal (for which the bombs were probably aimed) Aitchison Blair's factory in Stanford Street and a tenement in Livingstone Street were bombed fairly early on. At No. 69 Livingstone Street, which received a direct hit, the tenement collapsed and a young girl, nineteen years of age, was trapped for fourteen hours beneath the debris. She had been holding a neighbour's baby when the explosion occurred and she was thrown underneath the sink. The child unfortunately did not survive the explosion. For five hours men of a rescue party worked hard to release the trapped girl, who talked cheerfully to them although in great pain as her legs were crushed. At last an A.R.P.

Warden, who was of small build, managed to crawl through and rescue her.

In the Parkhall area, the Wardens on patrol saw incendiaries falling first in what were then the open fields near Braidfield farm and thereafter several showers of incendiaries dropping down on Singer's coup and on Parkhall itself. In Parkhall, some of the residents in Chestnut Drive had earlier in the evening been actually considering how to raise funds to purchase stirrup pumps. When the incendiaries fell in their street and gardens they did their best to deal with them by throwing dust-bin lids and even the dust-bins over them so that fires did not spread. The district was left in comparative darkness and little damage was caused by fire except in Sycamore Drive and Rowan Drive.

Clydebank Ablaze

The mission of the German pathfinder force to start fires which would serve as markers for the follow-up aircraft was accomplished with a considerable degree of success from the German point of view: and the fires which began then determined the pattern of the later bombing. The effectiveness of the incendiaries was largely, if not entirely, dependent on the accident of where they fell. Generally, at industrial sites where the structures were of brick, concrete and metal, incendiaries caused comparatively little damage. But in the Clydebank area two of the first fires started were at industrial sites full of inflammable material—Singer's timber yard and Yoker Distillery, just over the boundary with Glasgow. In the forty acres of the timber yard belonging to the Singer Manufacturing Company, engaged during the war in the manufacture not only of sewing machines but also of armaments, including the Sten machine guns, a vast store of wood, estimated as worth at least £500,000, and, in addition, Government stocks of timber of unknown value stored there, were completely destroyed by fire. Yoker Distillery, one of the oldest in Scotland, was on the other side of Yoker Burn from Clydebank but the flames and smoke were to attract to the eastern portion of Clydebank the later German bombers, who were not looking for specific targets but just dropped their bombs on or near the fires. In the eastern parts of Clydebank, even as far west as Radnor Park, the aroma of whisky from the Distillery was already evident in the small hours of Friday morning.

Another huge blaze which was to attract the attention of the later arrivals of Luftwaffe units occurred early on at Radnor Park School on Kilbowie Road. It was not the only school to be burned down on that night and the following night. Boquhanran School, not so far away from Radnor Park School, was another early victim to the German incendiaries. Clydebank High School's old building on Kilbowie Road and St. Stephen's School, Dalmuir, were completely gutted on the first raid along with Radnor Park and Boquhanran Schools, while Clydebank High School's new building on Miller Street, Elgin Street School, Our Holy Redeemer's School, Dalmuir School and St. Stephen's School's old building were partly wrecked. In addition, Duntocher Public School and Gavinburn School at Old Kilpatrick (where a large quantity of school furniture was stored) outside the Burgh were completely gutted and all the schools in the district had extensive damage to glass and plaster. The fires in schools were almost inevitable: most of them had large traps for incendiaries on the roofs, with central halls which provided a strong through draught and pitch-pine floors which burned well. Churches, like schools, fell easy prey to the enemy's onslaught by fire. Boquhanran Church and St. Stephen's R.C. Church, Dalmuir, were destroyed, while Radnor Park Church and St. Columba's Episcopal Church were badly damaged.

It has often been remarked about the German raids on Clydebank and other industrial towns that the industrial targets were missed or suffered little but the table in Appendix D shows the very extensive damages to industrial establishments in March, 1941. Although, as has been pointed out already, industrial buildings were less likely to be inflammable than schools or churches, serious fires developed in the two nights of the raid in Singer's timber yard, in John Brown's ship-yard, in Rothesay Dock. At the last place a store full of rubber caught fire and the smell and smoke of it drifted over the lower part of Clydebank. The Royal Ordnance Factory, Dalmuir, and Turner's Asbestos Works, where a huge 1000 kilo bomb fell, were also seriously damaged by fire. Not far from Clydebank, on its western boundary, three of the 70-80 Admiralty oil tanks at Dalnottar and Old Kilpatrick were bombed by the Luftwaffe and one of them set on fire. (The next night, when this tank was still ablaze, ten more tanks were set on fire, eight at Dalnottar and two at Old Kilpatrick.) Clydebank's blazing infernoes were of such magnitude that they could be seen by R.A.F. planes at Dyce near Aberdeen. It is little wonder that the later units of the Luftwaffe had no trouble in finding target area and concentrated on Clydebank, where the fires were, rather than on Glasgow.

Fire-fighting

As might be expected, the local fire services were overwhelmed by the calls made upon them well before midnight. Clydebank Fire Station remained intact but the three Auxiliary Fire Service Stations were put out of action early on, one being demolished and the others so badly damaged that they were evacuated. The telegraph lines were brought down and all telephonic communication with the Control Centre was disrupted for several hours. Worse still, of the three large water mains which brought water down to Clydebank from the hills, the largest, a 15-inch main on Kilbowie Road, was damaged at an early stage by a bomb, the other two mains, a 10-inch and a 12-inch, being put out of action in the next couple of days. The story of William Smillie, Sub-Officer in the Clydebank Fire Brigade, reveals the difficulties under which the firemen worked. 'I went to Second Avenue and saw three incendiaries lying on the road. I was earthing them over when I heard someone shouting: "For God's sake come and help us". A shelter had collapsed and there were men in it trying to hold the roof up with their backs. I put my crew in and ran for a rescue squad. A gas main was leaking and when I got back, four of my crew were unconscious. I got them to the stage where they were vomiting but on their feet and then we tackled a burning tenement in Montrose Street but before we'd got far with that a screamer came down and blew me over the wall into the churchyard unconscious. When I came to, the pump was dry: the bomb had taken half of Kilbowie Road and the big water main with it, and left Clydebank without water. The hydrant was dry, so we used the crater. I got the men together and we had another go at the tenement and then after that a four-storey tenement in Kilbowie Road and then some villas. We did those jobs and then we reported in.

'A call came in right away to say that No. 57 Livingstone Street was alight. I went there. No. 57 and every other number in Livingstone Street was alight. It was a great place for lodgers, which meant that nearly every room had a fire in it. Bombs had landed and blown most of the fires out on to the carpet. I was on the job there from Thursday to Sunday.'

Calls sent out to Glasgow and Dumbarton (both of which were also under attack early on) and to neighbouring local authorities brought 65 major units from other fire brigades into Clydebank before 4 a.m. on the Friday. At that hour, the Regional Fire Brigade Inspector, who had arrived from Edinburgh, decided to concentrate operations on Singer's timber yard, Rothesay Dock and the Radnor

Park-Kilbowie district.

Many of the outside fire brigade units were unable to function for a number of reasons. The regular fire brigades arrived in self-propelled engines which could not approach near enough to the scene of operations because of craters and the debris of buildings brought down by the explosion of bombs. Another serious difficulty which had already been experienced in English raids was the lack of uniformity or standardisation in hose-couplings at that time. (It was later stated locally that Clydebank's hose and hydrant couplings were different to those of the rest of Scotland but actually there was no uniformity either in the rest of Scotland or England.) Many outside fire brigades could not use their own hose for extensions or were unable to fix them to the fire hydrants. Even if they were capable of being fixed, the fire hydrants could not easily be found as in 1941 they were not painted yellow to distinguish them as is done today. The Forth and Clyde Canal however was convenient to Singer's timber yard and to the sites of some of the other fires, and the outside fire brigades with the large pumps drew their water from the Canal or from the static water supply emergency tanks. The smaller trailer-pumps of the A.F.S. could be manhandled near to the location of the fire but this advantage was to a large extent offset by the fact that these pumps had a much shorter throw of water. The fire-hose also was in many cases damaged by being hauled over debris containing glass and sharp stones. Nevertheless all the local and outside units were manfully carrying on at 10 a.m. on the Friday. At 2.45 a.m. the Clydebank Firemaster had sent a message to the U.C.B.S. for tea and rolls for 150 firemen, and these were taken at great risk to life and limb by a U.C.B.S. baker, Matthew Myles, in his van to the Town Hall. But otherwise, apart from some more tea and rolls brought round by mobile canteens in the morning, the firemen had been working continuously and many were nearing the stage of exhaustion. Some of the firemen from outside fire brigades returned home in the forenoon while others were brought in. But at 3.30 p.m., when 23 pumps were still engaged, it was obvious that the fires would not be under control before nightfall.

Lord Rosebery, the Scottish Regional Commissioner for Civil Defence, arrived from Edinburgh at 8 o'clock on Friday morning. It was impossible to make a proper appreciation of the situation but it was obviously one of considerable magnitude and difficulty. Rosebery visited, in addition to other places, Rothesay Dock, where there were two major fires, one of them at that time completely unattended, and he then formed the opinion that the fire-fighting operations lacked proper direction. When it became known early on Friday evening that the German radio beam was directed on Clydeside and another raid was imminent, Rosebery ordered that the Clydebank Firemaster, Robert Buchanan, should be temporarily superseded by the Second Officer of Paisley Fire Brigade. Buchanan himself was naturally very hurt by his being superseded during the raids and tendered his resignation to Clydebank Town Council at the monthly meeting in April following the 'Blitz'. He may also have taken upon himself the blame or some of the blame for the failure to overcome the fires of March 13-14. His was a task, however, which was impossible because of factors outwith his control; and there is little doubt that no firemaster and no fire service could have coped with the inferno that existed in Clydebank on the first night of the 'Blitz'. The fires of the second night, although not so large, proved no less difficult to deal with under a different command, even with the assistance of fire brigades and units from all over Central Scotland and with knowledge of the experiences and conditions of the first night's raid. On occasions when catastrophes of such magnitude as that of the Clydebank 'Blitz' occur, the central government officials tend to assign the blame and responsibility to the local authorities and in this case Buchanan was made the scapegoat. He had had a serious illness in December, 1940, and did not live long to enjoy his retirement after this unfortunate end to a long and useful career, dying in his native Vale of Leven in October, 1941.

Bombs and Mines

Fires constituted the most serious threat to property during the Clydebank 'Blitz' but they would not have caused so much damage were it not for the effects of blast resulting from the explosion of bombs and parachute mines. The high explosive bombs and mines made it difficult for the fire-fighters to extinguish incendiaries and vastly extended the area of burning by reason of the blast. The total of 272 metric tons of high explosive bombs which the Germans claim to have dropped on Glasgow and Clydebank on March 13-14 was made up as follows:

	1000 kilo bombs, H.E.			4
	500 ,,	,,	,,	51
	250 ,,	,,	,,	335
(delayed action)	250 ,,	,,	,,	50
	50 ,,	,,	,,	497

'A' bombs (parachute mines)   42
'B'   ,,   (oil bombs)   101

(In addition there were 1,630 containers of incendiaries, each of 250 kilos in weight.)

There is a list of the number of bombs which actually fell in the Burgh of Clydebank, drawn up by the Royal Engineers Bomb Disposal Squad officers and the Burgh Surveyor's department and printed in Appendix F, but it covers the two nights of the German raids, and it is not possible to estimate what proportion of the bombs listed above fell on Clydebank on March 13-14. It must be remembered also that the rural areas surrounding Clydebank received many of the bombs perhaps originally intended for the burgh, but aimed by the German bombers at the decoy fires west of Cochno or the oil tanks at Kilpatrick or just dropped quickly anywhere near Clydebank in order to get away out of the danger zone and back home to base.

District		H.E. bombs	Parachute mines
Old Kilpatrick and Bowling,	1st night	70	3
,, ,, ,, ,,	2nd ,,	55	2
Duntocher and Hardgate,	1st night	32	12
,, ,, ,,	2nd ,,	70	13
Kilpatrick Hills,	Two nights	132	0

In addition, 17 unexploded bombs were found in the Kilpatrick Hills (and there might well have been more, still undiscovered), which would indicate bombs dropped in a hurry.

The official list of bombs dropped in Clydebank Burgh referred to above includes the raids of May 5-6 and 6-7, when the Germans directed their attention mainly against Greenock and Dumbarton and when 17 high-explosive bombs fell on Clydebank and also two parachute mines, the first of which fell on John Brown's playing-field at Barns Street, and the other, lifted by the blast of the first over the houses, fell in the marsh between Dunmore Street and Elgin Street. For the raids of March 13-14 and 14-15 the totals were: 428 high-explosive bombs (44 of them unexploded) and 13 parachute mines (8 of them unexploded); but a footnote explains that exploded parachute mines have probably been recorded as high-explosive bombs, and there is some doubt also about the accuracy of the figure for unexploded bombs, some of which, undetected then for a variety of reasons, may still be lying many feet below the ground.

Major Incidents

Most of the fatal casualties in Clydebank occurred as a result of the explosion of bombs and mines, either directly by blast or by the collapse of the building in which people sheltered. Hardly one street in the burgh was without a fatal casualty but some streets were affected worse than others. Second Avenue, where a direct hit 'pulled the face off Second Terrace' (to quote Mrs. Janet Hyslop, Head Warden of 'E' Group) and brought the whole front of the building down, was the street with the highest number of fatal casualties—altogether, 80 deaths at Nos. 72 to 78 and 159 to 163. They included ten of the Diver family in No. 76 and eight of the McSherry family at No. 161. Other major incidents involving serious loss of life occurred at Pattison Street (43 deaths at Nos. 7, 9, 10 and 12), Jellicoe Street (31 deaths at No. 78), Glasgow Road (20 deaths at Nos. 425, 431 and 433), Napier Street (27 deaths at Nos. 2 and 4), Radnor Street (23 deaths at Nos 60 and 62, including nine of the Richmond family at No. 60). It was in 78 Jellicoe Street that fifteen members of the Rocks families perished, the most grievous tragedy of the whole 'Blitz' in Clydebank; and to the present day the notice by the survivors of the families in the 'In Memoriam' columns of the *Clydebank Press* brings back recollections of that night of terror in Jellicoe Street. Among many rumours which circulated through Clydebank, Dumbarton and the Vale of Leven after the 'Blitz' was one about the deaths of over a hundred lodgers in the Benbow Hotel, Dalmuir, a working-men's hostel which received a direct hit; but actually only five men died. Of the 528 persons finally admitted as killed in the Clydebank 'Blitz', fewer than 50 died on the second night's raid, which gives some indication of the terrible ordeal suffered by the people on the first night.

Pattison Street was one of the streets in Dalmuir which were heavily bombed, presumably as they lay between the blazing Singer's timber yard on the one side and the Royal Ordnance Factory and Beardmore's Diesel Works on the other. The closes in the street were strutted and there were also brick or reinforced concrete shelters in the back courts but as these were damp the people preferred to stay in their own houses. As the raid developed, John Watson, tenant in No. 12, who had come back from Beardmore's Diesel Works where he had been on the back-shift (2-10 p.m.), tried unsuccessfully to persuade his family to go into the shelter; and at last, when the raid was developing in intensity, all the nine families in the upper flats of No. 12 went into the three bottom flat houses.

At first, Watson's two daughters found themselves separated from their parents but soon joined them in the centre ground floor flat, a room and kitchen, and huddled there in the small hall to be away from flying glass while bombs were dropping all round. At last came the horrifying impact of a high-explosive bomb on No. 12 Pattison Street, and the building collapsed on top of the tenants sheltering there. Fourteen neighbours in the adjoining ground floor flat were killed but all in the right-hand flat and all but one in the centre flat were saved. There the eight survivors, however, were trapped until the beams lying on top of them were pushed apart and they managed to crawl through to safety. They immediately 'dived' across the road through No. 11 Pattison Street to the shelter at the back but had hardly got inside when a bomb fell nearby and the ground heaved. The bomb had scored a direct hit on the shelter behind the pend at No. 5 and almost all in it were killed.

The last bomb fell just after 5.30 a.m. and the 'All Clear' sounded at 6.25 a.m. The Pattison Street survivors and others all over Clydebank, many of them now homeless, emerged from their shelters to see the town shattered and burning. Tenement buildings were gaping open as if a huge knife had sliced off one side; and at piles of debris rescue parties were already working away to extricate the living and the dead. Almost every road was impassable at one point or another: the Fleming family from Cedar Avenue, like many others in Dalmuir West who lost their homes, made their way to the Town Hall by Mount Blow Road, the Boulevard and Kilbowie Road, where the water-mains had been damaged by a direct hit and the tram-rails reared up to the sky in distorted shapes. The Watsons from Pattison Street, on their way up to Radnor Street to see about a relative there, saw the bodies of the killed people, covered in blankets and laid out along the pavement in Second Avenue as they passed along. At a W.V.S. mobile canteen in Radnor Street they were handed cups of tea, most welcome after their long night of terror. There they met some people who had spent the night in the open, in Boquhanran Park (or 'The Hielan'man's Park,' as it was more familiarly known). These persons were glad to be alive as they had gone through the most harrowing experience, bombs dropping all round them and on the houses of their friends and neighbours. A senior police officer, who also came on the scene just at dawn, described it as 'a pathetic sight'. He went on:

'Although the night had been fine those people sitting or lying on the open ground without shelter of any kind must have suffered severely from exposure. I noted that many of the women who owned one were wearing their most precious possession—their fur coats, no doubt snatched up as they left their homes to depart they knew not where'.

The 'trek to the hills,' which many on Clydeside practised during the air raids, did not, as it happened, lead people to a safe area, as the Germans dropped their bombs indiscriminately towards the end of a raid and also aimed them at the decoy fires west of Cochno.

Casualty Services

Among the early casualties of the 'Blitz' were the Casualty Services themselves: First Aid Posts and Depots were bombed and telephone communications disrupted. But nevertheless the First Aid and Ambulance units carried on and performed nobly amid the holocaust. As Thursday night was a practice night, most of the personnel were available when the siren sounded and a few additional volunteers turned up shortly afterwards so that from the start of the raid there were 12 First Aid Parties, 13 Ambulances and 13 cars available, while all the First Aid Posts were sufficiently staffed. As the raid went on, reinforcements from outside the burgh were summoned but only six First Aid Parties were able to reach the town because of bomb craters and unexploded (presumed to be delayed-action) bombs making the roads impassable.

The First Aid Post in Elgin Street School was damaged by blast from a parachute mine and much of the equipment rendered useless early on. The electric light failed and the water supply was cut off but sufficient medical supplies were transferred to the school playground shelters where over 190 cases were attended to during the raid. As the only light available was that of hurricane lamps, the cases were transferred as quickly as possible to the Blawarthill Hospital and, when it was filled to capacity with cases from Glasgow and Clydebank, to Canniesburn Hospital and others.

Boquhanran First Aid Post in Boquhanran School was also struck fairly early on by high-explosive bombs and incendiaries. Stretcher cases, walking injured in blankets, first-aid kits were first taken into the school shelters in the playground when the upper storey of the school caught fire. As access to Boquhanran School was becoming increasingly difficult, one of the ambulances attached to the Boquhanran First Aid Post had already been directed by a young messenger, William Sharp, to take casualties to the new High School building at Janetta Street, which was used as the Wardens' Control Centre for 'D' Group. The Commandant at Boquhanran, William Smith, who kept magnificently cool throughout the night's ordeal, first directed two volunteer nurses to attend to the casualties at the Janetta Street School; and then, about 2 a.m., during a lull in the bombing, decided to evacuate all the cases there. The new school building soon had its east corridor lined with stretchers, and walking injured, some accompanied by relatives, including children, crowded the adjacent corridors and stairs. Because of the fire hazard, some of the First Aid personnel were organised into fire parties to patrol the huge building and managed to extinguish incendiaries which fell on the roof and on the playground. The second night's raid, as we shall see, was to be as full of incident as the first for the Boquhanran casualty services.

Hugh Campbell, the ambulance driver from the Dalmuir depot, who was awarded the O.B.E. for his services, has already been mentioned in connection with the beginning of the air raid. Ambulance drivers and First Aid personnel performed wonders in answering calls for assistance as they had to proceed under heavy bombardment along roads which might turn out to be impassable or contained bomb craters which had to be cautiously circumvented. Another whose bravery was recognised by the award of the O.B.E. was Mary Haldane (now Mrs. George Allan), an ambulance attendant. She was travelling along Livingstone Street in an ambulance when a high-explosive bomb went off not far away and as a result of the blast the ambulance was blown on its side. Another ambulance, loaded with casualties, was destroyed, some of the occupants being killed and others injured. She extricated herself from her own ambulance with some difficulty and went to the assistance of the injured, taking them into a shelter where she gave first-aid treatment. Mary Haldane, whose own home was destroyed, remained on duty throughout the night and the next two days.

Those who were members of the A.R.P. and Casualty Services were unanimous after the raids in praise of the messengers, generally youths connected with organisations like the Boys' Brigade and Boy Scouts. Mounted on motor-cycles, they had a task which was probably the most hazardous of all but to them it was an exciting adventure; and when telephonic communication was impossible on the first night, they had the added thrill of knowing that the messenger service was of supreme importance in the saving of lives. They managed to survive the 'Blitz' comparatively unscathed but one unfortunately was killed—Robert M. MacFarlane, who met his death in Broom Drive.

The Final Year Medicals

When Boquhanran School, with its First Aid Post, was set on fire, some of the casualties in the area made their way or were taken to the A.R.P. Post at the Radnor Park Church Hall in Radnor Street. This was the headquarters of 'E' Group, which had as its Head Warden, Mrs. Janet Hyslop. Mrs. Hyslop, who now lives in Windsor Crescent, had been for a short period a Town Councillor in Clyde-bank, having been co-opted in 1938 to fill the vacancy left by Finlay Hart, and she was the only woman Head Warden in Clydebank. Sixty casualties arrived in the Church hall just about the time it was realised that the telegraph lines were destroyed. Mrs. Hyslop's son, who had been at an apprentices' strike meeting in Glasgow and had not long returned, was a messenger and he was sent off to the Control Centre in Dumbarton Road for ambulances but only one came. He was sent out again but did not return before help arrived from an unexpected quarter. Some time before midnight (Mrs. Hyslop was unable to state the time exactly as, like most persons on duty, she was too occupied to notice the time) there appeared in the church hall a young woman who looked around, asked 'Is there no doctor?' and walked out again. She turned out to be a student nurse who had been off duty on the evening of Thursday and had stopped an ambulance near her home in Giffnock on its way to Clyde-bank. When she discovered what their destination was, she volun-teered to assist and after finding that the First Aid Post at Boquhanran School had been destroyed and that no qualified person was available in Radnor Park Church Hall, she went straight back up to the Glasgow Western Infirmary in the ambulance to secure assistance, taking with her a small baby in an apparently critical condition.

At the Western Infirmary, doctors and nurses were busy dealing with casualties brought in from bombed houses in Hillhead, Hyndland and Partick in the west of Glasgow, which also received the attention of the German bombers on the night of March 13-14. In the Infirmary there were also some medical students, whose final examination was only nine days away. They were supposed to turn out after a raid when the 'All Clear' siren sounded, in order to assist the various surgical units formed for such an emergency. Instead of waiting for the 'All Clear', however, they had made their way to the

Infirmary before midnight, when it became apparent that a heavy raid was in progress; but, as so many doctors were present, the students were assigned the frustrating tasks of merely writing down details of injuries received, etc. One of these students, dressed in his white coat, was approached by the young nurse who had carried the baby from Clydebank and she asked him: 'Doctor, is this baby dead?' The baby was still alive, fortunately, and survived the night. When the nurse told her story about the church hall in Clydebank, full of injured people without medical aid, the student mustered a few of his colleagues, who received permission from their surgeons to leave on their mission of mercy. The Medical Superintendent, Dr. MacQueen, was asked for medical supplies, including morphia, but he refused absolutely to help and further declared that he would accept no responsibility for any action the students took. Undaunted, the students approached a nursing sister, Miss Isabella MacDonald, who immediately provided a comprehensive range of medical requisites, tied up in eight bedsheets like washerwomen's bundles. Morphia, however, was not included as Sister MacDonald was not prepared to defy the Superintendent's authority in this respect.

The journey to Clydebank by the Boulevard was not uneventful. Their ambulance, equipped with dimmed and hooded lights, at one time hit what turned out to be an unexploded parachute mine at Knightswood, and all the occupants were thrown about. At the same spot, on the return journey was a crater in which a single-decker bus had dropped. Then, approaching Clydebank, they were stopped by a policeman, who said that they could not go any farther because of debris and unexploded bombs. When they explained their mission and asked for directions, he replied, 'Make for where the fires are greatest!' When they arrived at the church hall, the minister, the Rev. James M. S. McNaught, and some volunteers were doing their best to cope with the casualties, some of which were very serious. As the students entered the hall carrying their bundles of medical supplies, the word sped round the injured— 'The doctors have come! The doctors have come!'

For the students it was indeed a baptism of fire, as not only were they faced with very exacting cases requiring more than first-aid with only very limited medical and surgical supplies available but all the time bombs, high-explosive and incendiary, were dropping round about them and houses were collapsing not far away. Three makeshift ambulances, one of them the ambulance which the nurse had commandeered, provided an invaluable service in carrying casualties from the hall to the hospitals. When asked by one of the students if they would undertake the task, which involved driving along roads almost impassable in places with the constant risk of being shattered by the explosion of delayed-action bombs, the drivers all pledged themselves solemnly before God to do so, and right nobly did they keep their word.

At last, after the 'All Clear' sounded and the dawn broke, the students and the nurse started off on foot for Glasgow, two of them to face examinations in the Royal Infirmary. Before long a large Crossleigh car came along and they were given a lift. Almost immediately afterwards a delayed-action bomb exploded in a field in front of the car, great piles of earth and stones pouring down on top of them, fortunately without serious injury. The car was brought to a standstill by the blast and when the students emerged to examine the damage, they discovered that the edge of the bomb crater was only eighteen yards from the car.

In a letter sent to Bailie Ernest (later Lord) Greenhill and forwarded to Provost Low of Clydebank, the father of one of the students described the part played by the embryo doctors and ended his account of their experiences:

> 'At 8.30 a.m. they returned to the hospital, blood-stained and weary after having lived through what will most probably be the most terrible experience of their professional lives.'

As it happens, most of them, soon after qualifying, had to face even bloodier scenes during their service in the R.A.M.C. overseas, but none of them will ever forget that night in Radnor Park Church Hall. Of those who took part, five graduated at Glasgow University not long afterwards and are still alive and in practice—Dr. Alexander Jamieson, Dr. Sutherland MacKechnie, Dr. Alexander MacLachlan, Dr. L. G. MacLachlan and Dr. George Wilson. Unfortunately, it has not been possible to trace or identify the young nurse whose prompt action enabled the students to save so many lives. The denial of morphia to the students had its repercussions: as a result of their representations, it was agreed that in future final year students would be given authority to administer morphia to air-raid casualties.

Police

Probably no branch of Civil Defence in Clydebank suffered so much personally or were so continually under stress as the police force. Fortunately, none of them lost his life but fourteen of the regular force had their houses completely destroyed while six of the Police War Reserve were in the same position. In addition, twenty-seven regular policemen and four of the War Reserve found their houses so badly damaged as to be uninhabitable. Nearly all of them were on duty right from the start of the raid on Thursday evening and carried on throughout that night and the next but were allowed four hours' sleep on the Friday. For nearly all of them, this spare time was taken up in looking after their families who were in most cases without a place to sleep in and had to be evacuated to friends outside Clydebank or go to one of the Rest Centres.

Some of the police officers were involved in incidents when going on duty. Sergeant John MacLeod, who lived at 43 Albert Road, was on his way to take up duty when bombs demolished houses on either side of him. From one of them he heard the voices of children shouting and he immediately clambered through the ruins and rescued two of them. He then went to another wrecked house and from under the debris helped to rescue three children and their mother and bring out the body of another child. He took charge and assisted in other rescues while the raid was at its height and, when all casualties had been removed, reported to the police station for duty. The following night MacLeod was informed that an old man, bedridden, was in a house which had an unexploded bomb in the front garden. The sergeant went into the house and carried the invalid out to safety. Incendiary and high-explosive bombs were falling all the time and MacLeod arranged for the evacuation of the area. MacLeod, a native of Lewis, was awarded the George Medal for his great courage, initiative and devotion to duty. He later became Inspector and today lives in retirement in Helensburgh.

Charles Hendry, who was then a police constable, was one of a number of policemen who acted as despatch riders. He was on his motor-cycle on the night of the second raid when a parachute mine dropped on the street ahead of him, demolishing buildings on both sides of Dumbarton Road, including the A.R.P. Depot where stores such as petrol, sandbags, etc. were kept in what had formerly been the garage of Clydebank Motors, a local bus company. Hendry summoned a rescue squad on learning that some people were buried there and that there was a risk of fire or explosion because of the petrol. He was responsible for rescuing four men from the wreckage, including a fellow-policeman, Iain MacAulay, whom he carried 300 yards to the police station in Hall Street. While on duty as a D.R.

Dalmuir West Tramway Terminus

Leaving Home, Radnor Street, Clydebank

he was several times blown off his motor-cycle by bomb blast. Hendry, who was a native of Aberdeen and later became Sergeant, received the O.B.E. for his gallantry; he is now retired and still living in Clydebank.

None of the police fortunately was killed nor seriously injured although Constable Iain MacAulay (later A.R.P. Officer) was buried in the debris of the bombed building in Dumbarton Road referred to above and was off duty for a week. MacAulay, who was injured in the explosion in Dumbarton Road, had narrowly escaped the previous evening. When travelling down Duntocher Road with Inspector Alex. MacDonald (in a Wolseley car presented by a lady for A.R.P. purposes), a bomb exploded in front of them at the end of Hornbeam Drive, making a huge crater in the road; but oddly enough, the glass of the windscreen was sucked out instead of being blown in—a phenomenon that was observed in other cases during the 'Blitz'. One War Reserve policeman after two successive nights on duty went missing for two days and finally reported himself at Carlisle Police Station, unable to explain how he had got there—a case of shell-shock.

After the raids, the police played an important part in the devastated town. The population fell from over 50,000 to about 2,000 at one time and some of the Civil Defence services were almost halved through the enforced evacuation of homeless wardens and other personnel. The police, however, nearly all of whom had had their houses destroyed or rendered uninhabitable, had to stay put and for a time many of them slept on palliasses in the Education Office at the foot of Kilbowie Road. Some who were fortunate enough to obtain accommodation out of the town had to perform regular tours of duty but the homeless officers billeted in the Education Office had not only their regular tours of duty but also had to turn out for alerts which, as it happened, were rather frequent in April and May. In the immediate post-raid period, the police had greatly increased responsibilities. A number of delayed-action and unexploded bombs had been located and supervision of such sites had to be maintained. Delayed-action or time bombs, as they were called, had fuses operated by a clockwork mechanism and generally the delay was less than four days. Neighbouring houses had to be evacuated until the time bomb went off and also while Bomb Disposal Squads were defusing unexploded bombs. On the Friday morning, after the first raid, soldiers were sent in to guard buildings and help with traffic control; and this led to a rumour which, reinforced by a Home Guard commander's misinterpretation of the order, swept the town, to the effect that the military were taking over the town. The result was the start of a panic evacuation, which was fortunately soon halted by Ministry of Information vans touring the town and denying the rumour. Looting, which the soldiers were sent in to prevent, was non-existent for the first few days and was carried on at a much later period by some of the squads engaged in repairing the houses and by some smart Glasgow thieves who used furniture vans for the purpose.

The Chief Constable of the county, A. J. McIntosh, himself played a notable part during the raids. He was actually on a routine visit to Clydebank on Thursday, March 13th, to investigate complaints about the lights in John Brown's shipyard during air raids. It had been arranged that the air raid siren should be sounded and observer planes were to be sent up to report the lighting in the shipyard. At 9.10 p.m., minutes ahead of the pre-arranged signal, the sirens did sound and the puzzled Chief Constable before long realised that this was no practice siren but the real thing. He hurried off to the Control Centre in the Library basement and stayed there or in the Police Headquarters until Saturday afternoon. On the Friday evening when the second raid began, he found 500 women and children in the Town Hall hoping to be evacuated. He took the initiative of phoning the S.M.T. depot at Old Kilpatrick and asked the Inspector in charge to send as many buses as they could to Clydebank Town Hall, which request was complied with almost immediately. The bus drivers when they asked about the destination, were told to take them to the Vale of Leven or anywhere they could think of. McIntosh was himself later awarded the O.B.E.

Unfortunately for his reputation, the local Superintendent, William McCulloch, was at an early stage placed in a dilemma in which he had to choose between his duty to his family and his duty as a police officer. He was sheltering with his family in an Anderson shelter in the garden of his house at 16 Overtoun Road, Dalmuir, when a bomb fell, destroying the house and causing the sides of the shelter to cave in. McCulloch extricated himself and his family with great difficulty, and then, with bombs and parachute mines falling all over Dalmuir, decided to take the family away from Clydebank up to Windyhills, on the Duntocher-Bearsden road. His absence was unfavourably commented on by some of his colleagues and the next day, when Brigadier Dudgeon, Inspector of police forces in Scotland, visited Clydebank, the Chief Constable, after consultation with Dudgeon, decided to transfer McCulloch temporarily to Kirkintilloch, his place being taken by John R. Smart.

Control Centre

At the Control Centre in the basement of the Public Library, Henry Kelly, Town Clerk and Civil Defence Controller for Clydebank, and his staff were up until midnight doing their best to cope with the unprecedented situation with which they were faced. Their sixteen telephones were almost constantly receiving calls or issuing instructions; but the breakdown in telephonic communications soon after midnight left them with a feeling of helplessness. When Kenneth MacLeod, who was Depute Chief Constable of the County, arrived there with Inspector Latto of the Special Constabulary, he found the officials snowed under the weight of reports of incidents and calls for help from all quarters. According to MacLeod:

'Piles of messages recorded by the telephonists lay on the table, messengers were coming in and out, and it was obvious that the staff were overwhelmed by the demands made upon them.'

Kelly, the Town Clerk, was assisted in his duties as Civil Defence Controller by James A. G. Hastings, Depute Town Clerk, and William G. Thomson, Assistant Town Clerk. Of the three officials, only Hastings is now alive; he became Town Clerk of Elgin, then of Galashiels, where he now resides. Two of the three were always on duty or on call, which meant reporting immediately on the receipt of the preliminary or yellow warning (signifying the approach of enemy aircraft to the British coast). On the night of Thursday, March 13th, Hastings was off duty and not under obligation to report. He was with friends in Glasgow, whose telephone number had been left with the Town Clerk in the Control Centre: and it was actually the absence of a phone call and the continual barrage of anti-aircraft guns and bombing which made him decide, in the small hours of the morning, to get back to Clydebank. He had to make his way on foot from Kingsway, Scotstoun, through Yoker and, after walking along Dumbarton Road to Yoker, he was immediately struck by the changed scene as he entered Clydebank.

'Immediately I got to the Clydebank boundary, the whole scene was one of devastation. Actually, the very first building on the north side of the road was a public house called the Yoker Bar. It had been bombed and on the other side of it was Yoker Distillery and some of it was on fire. It is a ridiculous thing to say but if the German bombers had been briefed not to bomb

Glasgow and only to bomb Clydebank they could hardly have been more accurate at that end of the town.'

Before Hastings arrived at the Control Centre in Dumbarton Road, the telephones had all gone dead, the electrical supply had also failed and the pace of the Control Centre had dropped to almost nothing, the Control Centre being dependent on the youths who acted as messengers, and ambulance men, ambulance drivers and others, many of whom were acting on their own initiative in dealing with emergencies. Kelly, the Town Clerk, who had been badly shot up in the First World War and was subject to severe headaches, was nevertheless perfectly in command of himself and with the situation, or at least as much as that would permit. Within a few minutes of the arrival of Hastings, about 3 a.m., a German bomb hit the Library above the Control Centre and the whole building rocked.

'There was a most damnable crash above. We were showered with glass, which percolated through the wooden reinforcements (in the ceiling of the basement). No one was terribly concerned at the moment: we were alive and we shook the dust off our papers and equipment and got on with the job. The library itself was a perfect shambles.'

On entering the vestibule of the library next morning to view the damage, the Convener of the Library Books Sub-Committee, whose own home had been destroyed, picked up two books which had been blown towards the door. They turned out to be *Germany, the Last Four Years: An Independent Examination of the results of National Socialism* by Germanicus and *A History of National Socialism* by Konrad Heiden. The Town Clerk's office in the adjacent premises was also damaged by another bomb which left records and documents scattered about but caused no loss of life.

On Friday morning the District Controller for Civil Defence, Sir Steven Bilsland, set up what was termed Advanced District Headquarters in the police station (actually in the men's billiard room), which was staffed for several days by civil servants from the District Controller's Glasgow office. The Control Room under the library continued to function but Kelly himself, whose wife and family had been evacuated to Gartmore before the 'Blitz', and his depute, Hastings, slept for weeks on camp beds in their own offices or in the basement below. Kelly's own house was bombed in the second night's raid; and Hastings, who was in lodgings in McGhee Street, also found himself soon without a roof over his head. A number of houses in

Kilbowie had the roofs lifted by bomb-blast, and the roof-ties were in consequence loosened in addition to windows being shattered and ceilings having fallen down. Hastings was actually trying to persuade his landlady not to leave Clydebank when he nonchalantly leaned against the wall of the room they were in and the wall collapsed.

Friday's Respite

One of the first problems of Friday, after the first night's raid, was that of the homeless, feeding them, arranging for their evacuation, and dealing with their enquiries about relatives and friends. The weather was fortunately still beautiful and spring-like with a fair amount of smoke haze due to the many fires still burning. People tended to converge at first on the Town Hall and on the Rest Centres which had been arranged previously for the accommodation of homeless after raids. Of the ten Rest Centres, however, two had been destroyed and another rendered unfit by reason of fires nearby. Before long, most of the Rest Centres were filled with two to three times the number of refugees originally intended. For example, the Boy Scouts' Hall in South Douglas Street had to accommodate the people intended for the Rest Centre at the adjacent hall of Our Holy Redeemer's R.C. Church, which had been rendered unusable. The Boy Scouts' Hall, which had been scheduled to accommodate and feed 150, contained on the Friday between 300 and 400 and on the Saturday almost double that figure. During Friday, two ministers, a Public Assistance Board official and some voluntary helpers in the hall arranged to provide the bombed-out people with tea, bread and margarine; and some of them also went out to be served at mobile canteens, many of them run by the W.V.S., who had come from Glasgow and other places in Central Scotland. Another Rest Centre, in the Union Church Hall, was filled by Friday mid-day, with more people coming in. From a small kitchen, milk was handed out in small bottles by local school teachers who had volunteered to assist. Later, when military kitchens had been set up, soup and milk pudding, hot and of good quality, arrived in containers, and everyone seemed to get something to eat. School teachers in this Rest Centre organised the registration of those present, a very important procedure for later arrangements which might be made. In addition, Ministry of Food officials arrived in the late afternoon to issue emergency food ration cards in place of those destroyed. By that time, several thousands (the number is put between 2,000 and 10,000 and no check was made at the time) were leaving Clydebank or being evacuated, some trekking out of the town on foot, all their worldly goods in a pram or a 'bogey', and others in buses after waiting for hours in queues.

In the forenoon of Friday, Sir Steven Bilsland, the District Commissioner, who had set up an Advanced District Headquarters in the Police Station, decided that an Administrative Centre, to centralise arrangements for the homeless, should be established. This was done by members of the National Council for Social Services, mainly people from Edinburgh who had been called out in the early morning and had arrived in Clydebank about 11 a.m. after a stop in Glasgow. The first place chosen for the Administrative Centre, the Pavilion Theatre on Kilbowie Road (it was actually half cinema, half music-hall), proved unsuitable: it was blacked out and had a sloping floor and fixed seating. Officials started to distribute travel vouchers and billeting certificates in a passage-way upstairs, which soon became jammed by the waiting queues; and, after a while, it was decided to move across the road to the West Church Hall, where the Public Assistance Board and Ministry of Pensions officials were already operating. By one o'clock the transfer was made. Ministry of Information vans touring the town announced the opening of the Administrative Centre and soon people began to arrive in large numbers.

As it turned out, it is doubtful whether the opening of the Administrative Centre improved matters for the bombed-out people in the Rest Centre or for the burgh officials, as it led to a duplication of efforts. In the absence of any definite arrangements and of adequate staff, it soon became difficult to control the crowds, and there ensued one of those altercations between officials which occur on occasions of this kind.

A. M. Struthers of the head office of the National Council of Social Services and W. Ballantine of the Ministry of Information met Sillers, the District Commissioner's representative, in the Control Centre about 3 p.m. Struthers gives his account of the meeting:

'When we asked for definite information on the questions being asked, he (Sillers) waved a copy of the Department of Health pamphlet, "Information for the Homeless," and said, "It's all here". This left Ballantine speechless. He next wanted to know why we were setting up an Administrative Centre. It was explained to him that the decision was the District Commissioner's and not ours. We were merely trying to be helpful

in a very difficult situation for every one . . . There was a
similar pointless discussion with Sillers on the transport of the
homeless out of Clydebank that night. The reports from the
Rest Centres, as well as our own observations, indicated that
there was anxiety among homeless people. We wanted Sillers
to take action to ensure that the District Commissioner's decision was carried out, but he just sat, a perfect example of the
complacent official who regards voluntary social service
workers as busybodies who should mind their own business.'

Many of the Clydebank Burgh officials, who had been up all night,
were by this time almost dropping on their feet—the Town
Clerk, the Sanitary Inspector, the Burgh Surveyor, the Fire Master,
the Public Assistance Officer, all desperately coping with a situation,
unparalleled in their professional lives. Actually, many of the
problems confronting Struthers in the Administrative Centre in
Kilbowie Road were being dealt with by burgh officials in the Rest
Centres. Hastings, Depute Town Clerk and Civil Defence
Controller, made a tour of the town to assess the damage and sort
out priorities. Everywhere he went, he saw fires, with fire-engines
and fire-pumps standing by, immobilised for reasons given above.
On the outskirts of the town were reinforcement fire brigades unable
to proceed because of blockages on the roads. As Hastings saw it,
the first priority was for road clearance squads to get the main
arteries into the town cleared—Great Western Road (the Boulevard),
Glasgow Road, Dumbarton Road and Kilbowie Road. This proposal was quickly agreed to and the work put in hand. The second
priority was to obtain petrol for the fire-engines principally but also
for other vehicles. Local garage supplies, it was found, had been
destroyed or already drained so that the town was without petrol.
Hastings travelled up to Glasgow to the office of the Petroleum
Board in Bothwell Street to arrange for petrol to be sent to Clydebank but unfortunately his arrival there coincided with the office
lunch hour. After dealing with the office boy who had been left in
charge, he was told by an official he contacted by telephone to come
back in the afternoon—an example, he afterwards declared, of 'the
sort of peace-time easy-going attitude that I had experienced from
most of the Government departments at the time'. Fortunately, he
then remembered a petrol depot he had seen in the Port Dundas
area. This he contacted and was immediately assured that a lorry
load of full petrol cans would be in Clydebank as soon as he was.
By the middle of the afternoon the petrol was being distributed

among lorries, fire engines, etc., and from then on there was no difficulty about petrol shortage.

The possibility of another German raid that night was one which most people took for granted. It had been the usual practice of the Germans to raid large industrial towns on successive nights and the outlook for Clydebank was not encouraging. At Old Kilpatrick there was still one oil tank on fire, despite the efforts of hundreds of firemen drawn from near and far, and the smoke could be seen for miles. Up on Kilbowie Hill there were 'patches of torches', as they have been described, fractured gas mains which had been set alight in the previous night's raid. Attempts to enlist the services of the local repair squad failed as they had been 'bombed out', and Glasgow Corporation's Gas Department, which was actually responsible for Clydebank's gas supply, had too many jobs to attend to following the raid on Glasgow the previous night. The flames from these gas-pipes, sometimes 10-12 feet high, were to go on burning right through the day and naturally would prove good beacons for the German Luftwaffe, should it come, and come it did in earnest.

The Second Raid

About 6 p.m. on Friday, Goddard, one of the District Commissioner's 'link men' in Glasgow was sitting along with Hastings, the Depute Town Clerk, in the Control Centre when the telephone (the only one left out of sixteen) rang. Goddard picked up the receiver, listened for a moment and then put it down. After a brief silence he turned to Hastings and said: 'Well, they're coming back'. He then explained that 'the beam was on', meaning the German radio navigational beam for the aircraft of the Luftwaffe. Although, according to Civil Defence regulations, this information was supposed to be top secret and highly confidential to the Civil Defence Controller of the town to be bombed, in this case Kelly or his depute, Hastings, it was obviously foolish not to take action immediately to prepare for the night's onslaught. Hastings at once alerted the heads of services and arranged with them for skeleton teams to be kept handy in the centre of the town, particularly fire-fighting and rescue teams, and to send most of the units available to the perimeter of the burgh, in the Duntocher and Hardgate area, to be on call.

When the sirens went at 8.40 p.m., most of the much-reduced population left in the town made at once for shelters, although some again started their 'trek to the hills'. Again, it was a beautifully clear moonlit night but as the raid went on a murky haze developed from the many fires, especially from those at Dalnottar and Old Kilpatrick, where ten tanks were set ablaze. Over most of Central Scotland there was a slight fog in the morning which, according to the German reports, interfered with their bombing and, according to British reports, prevented any nightfighters operating. In all, 203 German bombers took part in the raid on Clydeside dropping 231 tons of high-explosive bombs and 282 incendiary containers over the same area as on the previous night but with an extension of the area two kilometers to the south-west, where a number of aircraft were briefed to bomb the Rolls-Royce works at Hillington. (It may be mentioned, in passing, that although incendiaries started a number of fires and high-explosive bombs damaged water-mains, production at the Rolls-Royce works was not affected.) According to the R.A.F. report on the raid, nearly all the German bombers came from the direction of Holland and crossed the east coast between Tynemouth and North Berwick, others from the direction of the Channel Islands proceeding over Lyme Bay, the middle of Wales and Burrow Head. One enemy aircraft went as far north as Aberfeldy before turning south over Glasgow. There were no enemy aircraft over Clydeside between 2 a.m. and 3.30 a.m. when aircraft came from Denmark, of which five went to Glasgow/Clydeside.

The total of 231 metric tons of high-explosive bombs (272 on the previous night's raid) was made up as follows (figures in brackets indicating bombs dropped the night before):—

	1,000 kilo bombs, H.E.			3	(4)
	500 ,,	,,	,,	42	(51)
	250 ,,	,,	,,	249	(335)
(delayed action)	250 ,,	,,	,,	15	(50)
	50 ,,	,,	,,	222	(497)
	'A' bombs (parachute mines)			54	(42)
	'B' ,, (oil bombs)			92	(101)

In addition, there were 781 incendiary containers, compared with 1,630 on the previous night. It must be pointed out once more that many of the above bombs were dropped in districts of Glasgow and in the landward area adjacent to Clydebank.

It may be observed from the list that the number of bombs of each type was smaller in the second raid, with the exception of parachute mines, and this was certainly the impression in Clydebank. One of these mines (cylinders of thin metal, about 8 ft by 3 ft, suspended by parachutes) landed about midnight outside the A.R.P. Depot in Dumbarton Road; the incident, involving the death of four persons in the building opposite (No. 131 Dumbarton Road), is recounted above in the section dealing with the work of the police. In Parkhall District, the new High School at Janetta Street (in use as a First Aid Post since Thursday night's raid) was hit by a parachute mine at the west end and the walls there caved in. Fortunately, the explosion was well away from the stretcher cases which had been laid down near the Janetta Street door. Later, a messenger came in to report that the Wardens' Post (on the site of the present Parkhall Branch Library) had received a direct hit and a number of people sheltering in it had been killed or injured. A rescue team from Helensburgh assisted in bringing out the casualties, which included eleven killed. In the higher part of Parkhall, the fight against incendiaries was more difficult than during the first raid with no water supply available. Robert Elder of 44 Chestnut Drive, an A.R.P. Senior Warden in 'D' Group, found the roof of his own house on fire and used the axe of one of the A.F.S. firemen to cut away the burning beams, forgetting that there were still gallons of water in the storage tank in the loft. The adjacent block of houses, like many others, was burnt to the ground.

More than one eye-witness has testified to some of the German raiders dive-bombing through the murky haze on this second night's raid. One came down towards the Town Hall so steeply that observers were sure it was going to crash but at the last moment it pulled out of the dive and sailed across Dumbarton Road, not much higher than the Municipal Buildings. Other eye-witnesses claim to have seen machine-gun bullets spattering the streets and the buildings in Dalmuir. Although the total death roll on the second raid was under ten per cent of that on the first raid, for some the Friday night was worse in that they lost their homes (as did the Town Clerk, Henry Kelly) or their loved ones or both.

Rescue Parties

The war-time establishment in Clydebank of eight rescue parties, of which four were full-time paid personnel, was early on found insufficient to deal with the numerous calls for assistance for people burried in the debris of bombed houses. At 11.15 p.m. on Thursday, March 13th, the Clydebank Control Centre sent a message to the County Control Centre at Dumbarton, asking for eight rescue parties which were quickly sent. By 3.30 a.m., when buildings were still being blasted by high-explosive bombs and almost immediately going up in flames, the Control Centre asked District Headquarters in Glasgow for eight more rescue parties, which were supplied from Stirlingshire and arrived without delay, despite the numerous blockages on the roads leading into the town. On the second night's raid, Clydebank Control Centre was again forced to ask District Headquarters before midnight for assistance, on this occasion for eighteen rescue parties, all of which arrived long before daybreak. The work of these rescue parties was stated in an official report to have been beyond all praise. As far as can be ascertained, they managed to relieve all those trapped alive in buildings except where they were forced to abandon their task because of fire. One of the difficulties which faced them and which led sometimes to a loss of valuable time was the uncertainty of neighbours as to whether people were trapped or not.

Some of the Clydebank rescue parties were on continuous duty for about three days. Two of the foremen received the well-deserved award of the George Medal for the parts they played in saving lives. James Gray, who was employed in the Burgh Surveyor's Department, was one of those on duty continuously for 72 hours. At one incident, where a tenement property had been partially demolished, a young woman was trapped in the basement. Gray tunnelled through the debris notwithstanding that fire broke out twice during the operation. He succeeded in jacking up the joists and after working continuously for a period of nine hours, during which he refused to allow any of his party to relieve him because of the danger, he managed to rescue the woman alive.

Another foreman, John Stewart, also a burgh employee, had a similar task to perform in a building also partially demolished and on fire. Stewart crawled through a small opening he had made and rescued several persons from the wreckage. Shortly before the last was rescued, the walls of the building collapsed.

Two other foremen received the O.B.E., David Logan and John Smith, who were like Gray and Stewart employees of the Town Council. When informed about his decoration, Logan, speaking for both, gave praise to their assistants: 'We had marvellous squads; the boys all did well and worked like niggers.' Logan told a story during this interview about two unknown heroines of the 'Blitz'. 'They were bus conductresses of about twenty. They were working with us, helping injured, when a heavy bomb fell less than 50 yards away. They were carried off their feet by the blast but they showed no fright. They scrambled up again and set to work with a will to deal with some of the more severe casualties. I hope their story will be printed and that they will read it to know that someone has not forgotten the glorious work they did that night. They are the unknown heroines of the "Blitz".'

An interesting story of one of the outside rescue parties concerns the party that went amissing. It was composed of miners from some town (?Bathgate) in West Lothian. They arrived on the Friday and were sent to deal with the results of an explosion in Mount Blow. Rescue parties from outside the burgh were supposed to return to their depots after twelve hours, and on the Monday or Tuesday, when they had not returned, a telephone message was sent by the burgh surveyor of their town regarding their whereabouts. It was quite a mystery for the Clydebank officials, although understandably in the confusion of the raids no proper check had been kept of the numerous rescue parties from outside. Then one of the officials remembered having seen a tunnel which looked like miners' work, in some debris not far from the church near the canal bridge at Dalmuir. Sure enough, there they were! They had built for themselves a hut out of pieces of timber and, when discovered, they were brewing up some tea before going on to another job. When told about the message from the burgh surveyor, they replied that they would return when they heard that their own town had been bombed and that they were required, but otherwise they would stay as long as they were needed in Clydebank. These miners had a different technique from the other rescue parties, which generally tackled the rescue of buried people by standing on top of the debris and gradually throwing it off, whereas the miners constructed a little tunnel, about two feet high, from the street through the wall of the building and thereby got into the centre of the debris to the space where the people to be rescued were. One tunnel made by the miners was kept in being for some time as a kind of showpiece; and in the long run their method was recommended by the authorities in their manual of instructions.

Ack-Ack and Nightfighters

The British newspapers after air raids were unable, because of the war-time censorship, to give specific details about the location of bombed buildings or fires or the number of casualties. Vague expressions and circumlocutions such as 'In a tenement in a West of Scotland town' were used instead of, say, 'In Radnor Street, Clydebank'. The censors, however, did not seem to trouble with their blue pencils so far as statements of enemy aircraft destroyed were con-

cerned. The *Glasgow Herald* of March 15th, 1941, in its account of
'the raids on Central Scotland', referred to 'the barrage of anti-
aircraft fire which traced the paths of the aircraft as each battery
roared into action,' adding that 'it is believed two planes were
brought down'. With reference to night fighters, the newspaper
report stated that 'to many spectators the conviction was driven
home that at least one of the raiders was brought down fairly early
in the raid'. Such stuff was considered suitable for boosting the
morale of the civilian population and obviously did not reveal anything to the Germans which they would not be already aware of.
In fact, the claims in the press were partly true: no planes were
brought down by anti-aircraft (or 'Ack-Ack') guns but one
German aircraft was shot down by a nightfighter in West
Scotland and, in addition, another on the way to Scotland was shot
down off the Northumbrian coast.

The German official records dealing with British defences show
that on the first raid the German aircraft met with light and heavy
Ack-Ack fire between 10.35 and 11.49 p.m., which had 'varying
success', and, in the following night's raid, heavy and medium-heavy
Ack-Ack fire, 'some of it well directed'. On neither raid did the Germans report the loss of a plane due to Ack-Ack fire, although the
guns must have helped to keep the German planes at a fair altitude
and to shorten their stay over the target area. No one who lived
through the 'Blitz' in Clydebank seems likely to forget the terrific
barrage on the first night from Ack-Ack guns on a Polish destroyer,
which happened to be in John Brown's dock for repairs at the time.
The Polish gun crews may well have emptied their magazines as some
observers reported and it is possible that their fire did help to
protect John Brown's shipyard itself, which came off comparatively
lightly. (One apocryphal story, current at the time of the 'Blitz',
and related in all seriousness by a retired school teacher in 1974,
was to the effect that the Polish guns shot down one German plane,
the pilot of which, escaping by parachute, landed on the deck of the
Polish destroyer and that the Poles, without further ado, grabbed him
and threw him into the furnace.) The second night's Ack-Ack
defences were regarded both by Germans and by Clydebank people
as stronger. Four 3·5 inch guns at Duntiglennan farm had kept
popping away the first night until about 2 a.m. when the ammunition
ran out; and on the second night there were four larger guns at
Auchentoshan firing 4·7 inch shells.

Searchlights also played their part: they could be seen forming a cone with its apex following the enemy plane, in order to present a better target for the Ack-Ack guns and also to dazzle the pilots. The German Luftwaffe report on the second night's raid refers not only to the much improved Ack-Ack fire but also to the searchlights, 30-40 of them, forming a 'dome of light'. In addition, the German report mentioned 20-30 barrage balloons on Clydeside between 3,000 and 10,000 feet in altitude but it seems here that their estimates were much too high.

The German bomber shot down in the first night's raid in West Scotland was a Heinkel 111 on its way to the Clyde. Nightfighters were on patrol from Turnhouse airfield and Hurricanes, Spitfires, Blenheims and Beaufighters (30 in all) made 42 sorties during the night. Pilot Officer Denbigh, flying a Blenheim of 600 Squadron (City of London), made contact, using the new radar interception device, about 6 miles south of Glasgow with the Heinkel 111 which was flying about 150 m.p.h. at 12,000 feet. The time was 9.51 p.m. just after the first raiders had dropped their bombs. The Blenheim closed on the enemy and attacked from astern with a 15-second burst at 150 yards. The Heinkel was hit, turned to starboard and lost height. The Blenheim closed again and gave another 16-second burst at 100 yards. In all, 1800 rounds were fired. The enemy dived away, was seen to lose height and crashed near Dunure at 10.20 p.m. The crew of the Heinkel 111, which was carrying a full load of incendiaries, baled out and were taken prisoner. The Heinkel blew up and burned out on crashing.

The only other combat in Scotland on the first night's raid took place 6 miles north of Glasgow at 11.30 p.m. when a Spitfire of 260 Squadron attacked a German aircraft, fired 960 rounds but without any visible result, and no claims were made. The aircraft shot down in the sea off Amble in Northumberland was attacked about 10.15 p.m. by a Spitfire of 72 Squadron, with Flying Officer Sheen as pilot. It was a Junkers 88, and ten minutes later it crashed into the sea, leaving no wreckage and no survivors. On the second night's raid, because of ground fog, there was only limited fighter activity and no interception was made.

PART THREE

AFTER THE RAIDS

Dogs, Cats and Canaries

The 'All Clear' after the second night's raid sounded at 6.15 on Saturday morning. It did not signify that there would be no more German planes that day but that for the time being the country was clear of enemy aircraft. One German plane, presumably on reconnaissance or weather observation, came in from the Clyde estuary in the afternoon, flying at a great height and must have had difficulty in assessing the damage in the bombed areas, if that was the crew's task, because of the heavy pall of smoke over the Clyde valley.

When dawn broke, it was obvious that Clydebank had suffered a 'major disaster', to quote the official report sent from the Scottish Regional Commissioner, Lord Rosebery. Behind the main streets, Glasgow Road and Dumbarton Road, which had suffered comparatively little damage apart from windows everywhere shattered and ceilings brought down, there was widespread havoc. In the report mentioned above, special reference was made to the Radnor Park district, where the houses in street after street were 'completely gutted, with only the gables standing charred and gaunt,' while the Whitecrook, Kilbowie and Mount Blow housing estates, not so much affected by fire, were heavily damaged by high-explosive bombs and parachute mines.

One ghoulish spectacle to be seen in the empty streets and smoking ruins was that of dogs, some of them hysterical, roaming around where their houses had been and desperate for food and water. Dogs and cats became a minor problem in the first few days. Some of them began to form packs and one police officer, who came upon a small pack hunting in the darkness round the new High School building in Janetta Street, part of which was in use as a mortuary, confessed that the sight gave him an eerie feeling.

The S.S.P.C.A. was contacted on the Saturday but it was not until Tuesday, March 19th, that representatives of the National A.R.P. for Animals appeared. An animal clinic was opened on the following day in Kilbowie Road opposite the Administrative Centre; and later a receiving office for stray and unwanted dogs and cats was started at 305 Glasgow Road by a small group of ladies who had for years had a similar office in Glasgow. Nearly 500 animals were brought into this office and painlessly destroyed; and by the end

47

of the year the total destroyed was almost 1800.

On the Friday and Saturday mornings of the raids a not uncommon sight was that of a homeless family with one of them in charge of a canary or a budgerigar in a cage, which remained with them wherever they went—to the Rest Centre in Clydebank, to the Rest Centre in the Vale of Leven or elsewhere. In Clyde Street School, Helensburgh, which was used as a Rest Centre for some time, Dr. J. P. McHutchison, Director of Education for the County, saw one man asleep on the floor with his parrot perched on his chest.

Cats and dogs were not the only domestic pets which lost their owners. When Kelly, the Town Clerk, went up with Hastings, his Depute, to have a look at Kelly's bombed house, Dunclutha, in Dalmuir, about half a dozen canaries, singing in the spring sunshine, gathered round their motor car, which was parked in the street near the house.

Evacuation

The whole of Saturday saw a steady evacuation from Clydebank. Wilson Stewart of Gavinburn Gardens, Old Kilpatrick, who was a boy at the time, recollects 'the seemingly endless stream of people from Clydebank, bound for Dumbarton and beyond, with belongings in prams, carts, barrows, or carried on the backs of old and young, fit and obviously unfit people'. The trek on foot had started the previous evening after the raid began and folk who had survived the first raid decided not to risk their luck again. When some of these evacuees arrived at Dumbarton they asked to be allowed into the Burgh Hall in Church Street, which was designated as a Rest Centre and according to regulations was not to be opened until after the raid was over. As there was nowhere for the Clydebank refugees to go and as bombs were dropping also in Dumbarton, the Civil Defence Controller, Fergus Roberts, Town Clerk of Dumbarton, gave permission to open the Rest Centre. Palliasses, which had been stored in the balcony of the Burgh Hall, were carried down by some of the men and several hundred spent the rest of the night there. The official view after the Clydebank raids was unchanged so far as the opening of Rest Centres during raids was concerned. Fergus Roberts later attended a meeting of local authority representatives who were reminded of this instruction and he took the matter up with the Department of Health. He rebutted the official ruling with vigour: 'With this attitude I cannot agree and I trust that the Department will not advise any local authority to act in

The Morning After

Emergency Drinking Supplies

this manner. Such advice is worse than folly'.

It has been estimated that about 3,500 were evacuated on Friday by buses, 2,500 to the Vale of Leven and 1,000 to Helensburgh and Kirkintilloch. Hundreds, if not thousands, more went off on their own to stay with relatives and friends. By Friday evening, all the Rest Centres except two, were cleared when the air raids started. One was the Episcopal Church Hall, where several hundreds waited on Friday for buses which never came. On Friday night, some remained in the Rest Centre, while others went back to their 'blitzed' homes or stayed outside, and not a few were killed. On Saturday, Sir Steven Bilsland, the Civil Defence District Commissioner arranged for buses from Glasgow which took the exhausted people away. The other was a school which, at this distance of time, cannot be identified but was possibly the new High School Building at Janetta Street. Messages about Boquhanran School and Radnor Park School having been burned down had led the officials in the Control Centre to think that all the schools in that area had been destroyed and nothing was done about the request for bus transport received during the Friday. Early on Saturday morning, an A.R.P. Warden arrived at the Control Centre in Dumbarton Road to report that the people in the school had spent two nights there. Within half an hour buses were at the school in sufficient numbers to take all the homeless to join the thousands already in the Vale of Leven.

By the forenoon of Saturday, after the second raid, many made up their minds to leave the town, particularly after hearing the rumours, mentioned earlier, that the military were taking over control and evacuating the civilian population. Approximately 200 buses were used in a shuttle service to transport the homeless refugees of Clyde-bank—an estimated 7,000 to the Vale of Leven, 3,000 to Coatbridge, Airdrie and Hamilton; 1,500 to Paisley, Bearsden and Milngavie; 2,500 to other parts of Renfrewshire, Lanarkshire and Dunbarton-shire. According to the report of the Scottish Regional Commissioner for Civil Defence, dated April 3rd, there were, in addition to the 3,000 who were evacuated on the 14th and the 12,000 on the 15th, at least 25,000 homeless who left on their own accord by the 15th, so that by the evening of Saturday probably over 40,000 (out of a population estimated at well over 50,000) had left the town. The report added: 'At no time during the ordeal through which the town had passed or afterwards was there any sign of panic; all accounts agree that public morale was magnificent'.

In the confused situation, it was possible for families to be split up and sent to widely separated reception areas. For almost all who boarded the buses, however, theirs was an unknown destination: it might be Helensburgh or Bonhill or Kirkintilloch or Blantyre, and for some the whole course of their future lives was decided by the bus they boarded on Saturday, March 15th, 1941, in Clydebank.

Rest Centres

The first evacuees arrived by buses in the Vale of Leven on Friday afternoon. From the beginning of the war, the Vale of Leven had been designated as a neutral area just as Clydebank was an evacuation area and Helensburgh a reception area. No preparation had been made by Government departments; and the local authority, the Vale of Leven District Council and its officials—the Clerk, the Public Assistance Officer, the Sanitary Inspector, etc.—were given the unenviable, almost impossible, task at an hour's notice of dealing with hundreds of bombed-out families on the Friday and thousands on the Saturday. Schools and halls could be, and were requisitioned but no one had considered, even as a remote possibility, that large numbers of evacuees would sleep, eat and live there for a few days, far less weeks. As a result, conditions of over-crowding, bad from the outset, became chaotic and almost intolerable. Volunteers in the persons of school teachers, janitors, ministers, W.V.S., and A.R.P. personnel, in no wise trained for the task, found themselves responsible for the welfare of hundreds of men, women and children, many of them bereft of all their possessions except the clothes they stood in. All the equipment available at first in most of the 15 places selected as Rest Centres was cups, 100 for each Centre—but no spoons or other utensils, no food, no blankets and, in some places, no sanitation except one W.C. Plenty of bread and margarine was forthcoming from people living nearby but it took some time before the Public Assistance Officer could get authority from the Milk Marketing Board and the Ministry of Food to release for the Rest Centres, milk which the Vale of Leven Co-operative Society and a local dairyman, MacFarlane, were prepared to supply.

Saturday was, as might be expected, the most trying day for all concerned. In the South Church, Bonhill, where 250 persons were crowded together A.R.P. Wardens were in charge. Rolls and milk were provided at 10 a.m. for breakfast and the Co-operative Society, it was arranged, would supply pies, etc. for dinner. When by 1.15 p.m. none had come, the evacuees began to show signs of a spirit of solidarity that was to grow stronger in the weeks to come, and an evacuees' committee was formed with Mrs. Campbell of 35 Chestnut Drive as convener. There were only 100 cups and a medium-sized urn in the hall and people were arriving on foot all the time from Clydebank, walking through the smoky haze of Old Kilpatrick and only emerging into the clear sunshine in the Vale of Leven. By 2 p.m. Mrs. Campbell and the evacuees' committee had everyone served with cups of tea. Nearby, in Bonhill Public School, where there were 300 persons at mid-day and more arriving every hour, a university student was in charge. A doctor had been in attendance and several of the evacuees had been sent to a clinic. A not infrequent request here, as at other Centres, was for the repair of spectacles, which had been broken in the 'Blitz'; and many men spent part of the day searching in vain for shirt-studs, razors and razor-blades, the local shops being quickly denuded of their stocks of these small but very necessary articles. Two cwts. of turnips and carrots had been delivered at this Centre but there was no means of cooking them. At St. Mary's R.C. School, where the janitor was in charge, there were 400 persons, none of whom had more than one slice of bread and margarine since arriving the previous evening. There were 100 cups but no cooking facilities for the turnips and potatoes which had been delivered.

Improvisation by the amateur wardens took many forms. Through the good offices of Mrs. Rendel, wife of the Officer Commanding, the Artillery barracks at Dalmonach near Bonhill Bridge took over the cooking and service of meals for the adjacent Rest Centres in Bonhill School, Bonhill Institute and the South Church Hall, the evacuees trooping down to the barracks for meals. In Renton Secondary School, where the headmaster, Scott, his wife and four teachers came in as volunteers on the Saturday, they put on the tea urn and all the saucepans they could find to boil water. The cookery teacher had obtained two cwts. of potatoes and a supply of carrots, and from these prepared a supper for the evacuees that night, six of the women evacuees peeling all the potatoes. As there were only utensils for 100, the teachers asked some of the older children to go round the houses in the neighbourhood for cups, dishes, spoons, etc. and before long returned with sufficient utensils for 320 people and a parcel of sandwiches marked 'For the teachers'.

When the first batch of evacuees arrived in the Vale of Leven Academy about 4 p.m. on Friday, the teachers who had been asked to assist by the Clerk of the District Council had managed, with the help of senior schoolboys, to clear the ground floor rooms of desks, which were stacked at the end of the school hall. The 400 evacuees were distributed in the ten rooms, where they squatted on the floor, taking tea and sandwiches prepared in the domestic science room. During Friday night, when Clydebank was again being bombarded by the Germans, some bombs fell in the Vale of Leven and a few of the women evacuees, reliving their experiences of the previous night, became hysterical, their children burst into tears and dozens crowded into the hall but were persuaded after a time to return to their rooms. The arrival of blankets at the height of the raid helped to distract attention from the noise of the planes passing overhead and induce the evacuees to settle down. Shortly after midnight, the Warden or Leader (as he was designated), a principal teacher who had found himself in the position without being appointed and without even volunteering, saw a group of local district officials and councillors entering the school, presumably on a tour of inspection. 'Who is in charge?' they asked. His answer was 'You'; but, as he well knew, they had no more responsibility for the state of affairs than he had.

On the Saturday, there came a second contingent of refugees. Four hundred were assigned to the second floor and the gymnasium; others appeared at the door demanding admission but were dissuaded by some of the first evacuees. Among the numerous problems confronting the Warden, who got no sleep himself for several days and nights, were the conditions of women's lavatories, the supply of sanitary towels, the washing of babies and their nappies, the question of pregnant women (a baby was born in the headmaster's room in Clyde Street School, Helensburgh), and an epileptic who had a fit in the middle of the night and had to be removed to hospital. School teachers, with no teaching duties, found themselves engaged in all sorts of domestic chores—peeling potatoes, preparing sandwiches, filling babies' bottles, which the science teachers warmed over the bunsen burners.

Before long, room committees were elected, and room leaders had daily conferences with the Centre Leader or Warden on matters of general policy as well as grievances and complaints. Most of the evacuees were looking or hoping for private billets and at one time the Vale of Leven evacuees threatened mutiny on the question of non-allocation of billets when a rumour had been put about that by law no Rest Centre should keep evacuees longer than 48 hours. There were two aspects of the billeting problem: finding suitable billets and persuading evacuees to go to them, as it might mean splitting up a family or difficulties in travelling to work. The authorities tended to deal with the problem in the method most convenient from an administrative point of view. One method caused great wrath among the evacuees. Thousands of workers in John Brown's, Beardmore's and other works in Clydebank were transported daily in buses from the Vale of Leven. When the men were absent at work and not able to object if necessary, a bus would arrive at a Rest Centre to take the families to their (as yet unknown) billets. Such a move at the Vale of Leven Academy Rest Centre was stopped after a meeting of evacuees' representatives held in the local Communist Party rooms. A demonstration, several thousand strong, was organised to march to Clydebank Town Hall; it was met half way by Sir Steven Bilsland, who from his Rolls-Royce gave an assurance that families would not be broken up.

The question of how to clear the schools of evacuees was one which exercised the Education Committee as it wanted to have the schools back for the education of the local children and the children of evacuees. On Wednesday, March 20th, according to official estimates there were 3,500 in Rest Centres and 4,409 in private billets in the Vale of Leven. By March 27th, i.e. almost a fortnight after the first raid, the number in Rest Centres was reduced to 1,164, but the rate of clearing the Centres slowed down. On May 10th, Clydebank Town Council had a special meeting to consider a request from J. Hall, Secretary of Levenvale School Evacuees' Committee, requesting permission for a deputation of evacuees, who were threatened with eviction from the school. There is, however, no record in the Town Council Minutes of a deputation being received, and it is possible that the Levenvale School deputation was part of the large demonstration referred to above. Some evacuees found the comforts of the Rest Centre so acceptable that they were most unwilling to leave. Drake, the headmaster of St. Mary's R.C. School in Alexandria, solved the problem at last in a way which had never struck any of the other Wardens. Drake had a friendly, cheerful manner and when a hard core of evacuees were stating to him their determination not to go aboard the evacuees' bus, he agreed with them most heartily and said: 'You have a right to better than a bus. Don't you go unless they provide a taxi!' They agreed and he then sent for a taxi, which they entered without a second thought for an unknown destination. (A semi-autobiographical novel, recently published, *In His Fashion* by James Harris Saunders, gives a vivid picture of conditions at the Vale of Leven Academy Rest Centre, where he was Warden.)

Private Billets

Most people evacuated from Clydebank after the raids into Rest Centres spent at least some time afterwards in private billets. Some were very fortunate and the householders who put them up for weeks or perhaps months became their friends for life. In a letter sent by Thomas Kearns to a friend Patrick Diamond, describing the 'Blitz', he wrote:

'God knows, Patrick, we were ever so thankful to our Merciful Saviour that we are all alive and sound to tell the story. The wife, Margaret, the twins, Kathleen and Ellen, and Jim with myself are so far happy and contented down here in the beautiful Vale of Leven. Tommy and Willie are evacuated to Kirkintilloch, all right, just a misunderstanding we are not altogether, a kind of mix-up in the evacuation from Clydebank. We arrived quite safe in Alexandria. I guess you were here many a time in the good old football days. We like the place very well indeed and are billeted with very nice Catholic people, and they do their utmost to make us happy away from heartbreaking surroundings.'

Too often the evacuee family was regarded as a burden or an imposition, and the result was ill feeling on both sides. David Kirkwood, M.P. for Dumbarton Burghs (Dumbarton and Clydebank), always keen to act as champion of his constituents, raised in the House of Commons on May 29th the question of the conditions in which evacuees were billeted and declared that some had been treated as though they were criminals, citing as an example the case of a family of a father and mother with thirteen children living in a hut. Major Lloyd, M.P. for East Renfrewshire, the constituency in which the hut was situated, took the matter up as many of his constituents who were looking after evacuees were angered by Kirkwood's language. Lloyd produced in the House of Commons a letter from the mother of the family expressing her gratitude and appreciation of the way in which she had been treated. Actually, a small committee had been formed locally to look after evacuees and had done their best for the family of 15, who refused to be separated. The hut was substantially built, 40 ft. by 20 ft., with a new floor of Oregon pine covered with linoleum, formerly in regular use by Girl Guides and well supplied with water, electric light, gas radiators and sanitary arrangements. Kirkwood's sweeping criticism evoked numerous replies in the Glasgow press from householders who had been looking after evacuee families. At a public meeting attended by over 800 people on Sunday, April 4th, in which Sir Steven Bilsland and Joseph Westwood, Under-Secretary of State for Scotland, were the main speakers, one of the audience heckled Westwood about Clydebank people sleeping in garages in Milngavie, while large houses there were empty—a question which brought down the house. Kirkwood intervened to say that if big houses were available, they would be taken over; but his answer provoked a young man into shouting, 'What about your own house?' Kirkwood, who lived in Bearsden, next door to Milngavie, retorted that he had three families in his house at present. When the young man again interrupted, the M.P. told him angrily: 'It's nothing but ignorance on your part. Your kind all need a mob to support you.' Kirkwood continued to suffer interruptions during his proposal of a vote of thanks but these were due partly to anger over billeting and partly to his attitude to the non-recognition of shop stewards in the Royal Ordnance Factory, Dalmuir, which seemed to his critics inconsistent with his own record in the First World War.

During the weeks and months following the 'Blitz', Clydebank's Town Clerk was constantly receiving letters from homeless people asking if and when they could be given a house in Clydebank. Some of them reveal only too clearly the difficulties facing the bombed-out in their enforced exile from Clydebank. A former resident of Buchanan Street, Dalmuir, who had been evacuated to the Vale of Leven, had first spent two weeks in the Masonic Temple there with his wife and family before being sent to the Vale of Leven Academy, where he spent a further three weeks, during which time they slept on the floor of the hall. From there, he and his wife and the younger members of the family were sent to Cove with the promise of a billet there. On their arrival, his wife with the three younger members of the family were put into a wooden hut, while he and the four older children (three boys of 16, 18 and 19 and a girl of 21) had to seek accommodation elsewhere. Finally, they returned to live with a sister-in-law in Duntocher, where they were staying at the time of writing, nine of one family and nine of the other, sleeping on the floor for lack of beds.

For those who did not leave Clydebank conditions were little better. Mrs. Janet Hyslop, Head Warden of 'E' Group, and her family had been bombed out of their home at No. 7 Third Terrace and she and her husband were billeted in the house of ex-Provost Smart at No. 2 Drumry Road, while her two daughters were evacuated to Milnathort. When the second allocation of repaired houses had been made, she decided to write to the Town Council, as she had heard on two occasions councillors remarking how comfortable she and the others billeted at Drumry Road were. In a letter of June 16th, 1941, she wrote:

'They seemed to be under the impression that because we were in ex-Provost Smart's house we had the comfort he had. On the contrary, we have one room in which three adults, eat, sleep and live. No furniture except what we salvaged from the Warden's Post, i.e. forms from the Church Hall with palliasses for beds, a table and three chairs. The house is occupied by Wardens and members of the First Aid—15 in all. . . . All the windows except part of one are boarded up and none of them open, with the result that the place gets stuffy and is not conducive to good health.'

Mrs. Hyslop, with her husband and sixteen others, had slept just after the 'Blitz' in the Warden's Post in Graham Avenue. They used to wash in empty houses nearby, and the men going to work had breakfast in the Town Hall or the Co-operative. Mrs. Hyslop's story could be matched by those of numerous 'Bankies' and brings home to us today the ordeal, protracted and apparently never-ending, of Clydebank people after the 'Blitz'.

Post-Raid Problems

For those who were left in Clydebank after the mass evacuation, Saturday night came and went without an air raid and Sunday morning was again fine and sunny. But there was hardly a house standing which did not show some sign of damage: indeed it was later stated that only eight were undamaged and of the total of 12,000 houses in the burgh 4,300 were either totally destroyed or damaged beyond repair. Despite the fact that roads and railways had been bombed and some of them still blocked because of time bombs, many Glasgow people travelled down on the Sunday afternoon to see the ruins of the bombed town, much to the annoyance of police, soldiers, wardens and others on duty.

Water, gas, electricity had all been cut off, and two tons of candles and about 6,000 boxes of matches were sent to the town under a scheme previously prepared. Some thoughtful person, presumably a smoker himself, also arranged for the delivery of 70,000 cigarettes and 15 lbs. of tobacco. Gas (at low pressure) and electricity were restored by Saturday night but in many homes were not available because of damaged mains. As for water, it was some time before a normal supply was restored, as will be detailed later. In the meantime, water was brought in barrels from Glasgow. Public Assistance Board officials had been engaged continuously in their multifarious duties, including their main duty of relieving those in distress (and there were thousands). They eventually ran out of cash on the Sunday but were provided with £3,000 in £1 notes through the District Banking Adviser within two hours.

During the first few days after the raids there was hardly anyone in the burgh who was not dependent for food on mobile canteens, army field kitchens, Rest Centres or the Town Hall Feeding Centre. Preparations had been made by the Ministry of Food for towns which had suffered a heavy raid but not for one on the scale of Clydebank. Assistance came from voluntary organisations and neighbouring local authorities, however, and Ministry of Food officials saw to it that abundant supplies were made available. Glasgow Corporation's Education Department was responsible for providing hot meals, cooked in Glasgow and brought down in containers and these were served in the Town Hall, where the Ministry established a feeding centre for A.R.P. workers and the public (which meant everyone who came). Volunteers, members of the W.V.S., Boys' Brigade, school teachers and others served the meals. Domestic Science teachers from Glasgow, led by a Miss Murray, were soon providing hot dinners for up to 6,000 and breakfasts for 1,000. In a few days there was no shortage of food and the meals at the Town Hall were regarded as sumptuous repasts by people restricted to war-time rations—'The one bright spot in our lives—food galore and as much sugar as you wanted,' according to one man who had all his meals there. When the Ministry of Food at last told the Town Council they had to run it themselves, the allocation of foodstuffs was reduced and the Clydebank people were back on to normal rations—half-a-spoonful of sugar for a cup of tea. Naturally, local people blamed the Town Council for the decline in standards. To us today the sugar ration may seem unimportant in comparison with the major troubles afflicting the people of Clydebank—loss of homes, loss of all personal possessions, the deaths of friends and relatives. But just like the cigarette issue to soldiers in war-time, such comforts were beneficial to morale and their removal tended to create a sense of deprivation.

The Town Hall was to remain a communal feeding centre for weeks to come. At the beginning, it was supplemented by mobile canteens almost all run by volunteers, particularly the W.V.S. On the Tuesday following the raids, there were actually 42 mobile canteens in the burgh, and it was estimated that they supplied food for between 15,000 and 20,000 people. One observer commented that Glasgow's wrapped and sliced bread, at that time a novelty to Englishmen, proved invaluable to those who were preparing sandwiches; and it is mentioned in the report of the National Council of Social Services that all sorts of fillings served for the sandwiches, some of the Edinburgh ladies bringing through 300 tins of sardines on the Sunday.

Immediately following the first air raid, the Civil Defence Commissioner for the Western District, Sir Steven Bilsland, whose office was in Glasgow, set up an Advanced H.Q. in Clydebank at the Police Station in Hall Street (in the billiard room) and his officials remained there for over a week. Every morning at 9 o'clock Bilsland held a conference of Town Council officials and Government officials from the Department of Health, Ministry of Food, Ministry of Home Security, Ministry of Information, etc., and he saw to it that no civil service routines or regulations would impede the necessary measures being undertaken by the Council officials. He gained the admiration and respect of those around him during this period of crisis—'a man in a million,' as one of them described him. 'He was a very sympathetic listener, a man who made up his own mind and, having done so, he stood no nonsense from anyone.' His contribution to the rehabilitation of the devastated town can hardly be overestimated and it is not surprising that his war work earned him the title of Lord Bilsland.

The Town Council's own A.R.P. Emergency Committee was for the time being superseded. A number of the councillors had lost their homes and others were engaged in work of national importance. But Provost David Low came down to the Town Hall every morning and in matters which required the approval of a member of the Town Council he saw that there was no delay.

Bomb Disposal

One feature of life in Clydebank the first few days after the 'Blitz' was the activities of Army Bomb Disposal Squads and Naval Mine Disposal Squads. 224 UXB's (or unexploded bombs) were reported but on investigation as many as 130 were discredited. In his report, the Major in charge of the Royal Engineers, like professionals in other walks of life, severely criticised the amateurs, the wardens and policemen who had wasted the sappers' time when so many urgent cases were to be attended to. When the soldiers came to the stage of de-fusing the bomb (often a simple enough job performed by the officer or N.C.O.) the adjacent houses were evacuated in case of things going wrong. Evacuation of buildings was carried out by the police also where a delayed action bomb was discovered. These time bombs were called 'tickers' by the sappers, who used a giant stethoscope to listen for the clockwork mechanism. The maximum delay for a time bomb was 96 hours, after which period, if they had not exploded, they were treated as UXB's.

Parachute mines were the responsibility of the Royal Navy Mine Disposal Squads. Forty-six UXPM's were reported (there seems to have been a number of duplicated reports) but 30 were discredited or had already exploded and 16 were dealt with by the Navy. Like the R.E. Major, the navymen complained about lack of definite information about the location of the UXPM's, which involved unnecessary reconnoitring. When the naval squad arrived the men took their equipment over to the east of Kilbowie Road where most of the UXPM's had fallen, and two officers, accompanied by the Depute Town Clerk, Hastings, to show them the locations, went over to the west side. A parachute mine was a huge affair, about 8 feet by 3 feet constructed of light metal and suspended from a parachute. There was one of them just off Radnor Street hanging from a damaged gable by its parachute cords and swaying in the breeze. Because of its precarious position, the officers decided to detonate it by rifle fire, which one of them effected with his fourth shot. A terrific explosion ensued (the blast of a parachute mine was reckoned to cause damage to houses up to 400 yards away), with the officers and Hastings seeking safety behind an A.R.P. shelter.

Water Supply

One of the first blows suffered by the Fire Service was the loss of a water supply following the bombing of one of the largest water mains, a 15-inch pipe in Kilbowie Road, which had to be shut off to prevent flooding. A large bomb exploded in the centre of the road just north of the junction with Montrose Street and formed a crater about 30 feet wide and 12 feet deep, six yards of the water main being blown out, leaving the exposed ends of the pipe tilted upwards; and in addition tramway rails were broken and lay twisted across the crater. Fifteen feet of a sewer were also blown out, leaving the ends buried in the crater and 10 yards of an 18-inch gas main were displaced and the joints leaking.

This incident was but the first of a series of misfortunes which placed a severe strain on the local water department during the 'Blitz'. James McWilliam, assistant water engineer, as soon as he was informed of the damage, proceeded to close certain valves and open alternative feeds to ensure water for fire-fighting, and he continued with his work throughout the night amidst all the bombing. He was aware that his own house had been bombed but uncertain about the fate of his wife; nevertheless he carried on with his work during the next day. McWilliam, who himself received injuries from bomb shrapnel, was later awarded the O.B.E. Another employee of the Clydebank and District Water Trust, George Aitkenhead, a foreman, left his home just after 9 p.m. on Thursday when the alert sounded and did not see his wife until 23 hours later. All the time he was working like McWilliam to conserve the water supply. His knowledge of the water distribution system and, in particular, of the valves buried beneath debris proved invaluable during the period of repairing the water mains. Aitkenhead, whose home at 303 Kilbowie Road was destroyed by fire on the second night's raid, was given the King's Commendation for gallantry and devotion to duty.

Work on the 15-inch main was started on Friday, March 14th at 10.45 a.m. by two water repair squads from Glasgow and one from Dumbarton and a detachment of Royal Engineers. At first, it was feared that the damaged sewer pipe might cause contamination of the water supply but it lay much deeper than the water main and as the broken ends of the water main were tilted upwards, this also acted as a safeguard against contamination. The twisted tramway rails also presented a difficulty until men and plant were obtained from John Brown's to cut them away. All during Friday, buildings near the crater were still on fire and occasionally a delayed-action bomb exploded, sending showers of bomb fragments over the men working in the crater. On Saturday, after the second raid, the fires in the adjacent buildings were even worse than Friday and the work was called off until the R.E.'s were able to demolish the buildings. Work was resumed on Sunday and the pipes were laid in position ready for jointing when about noon soldiers found a 250 kilo unexploded bomb in a neighbouring shop. Apparently, the repair squad had known about it for some time and were willing to carry on but were ordered to stop. A Bomb Disposal Squad arrived from Glasgow and the bomb was finally exploded at 7 p.m. but a day's work had been lost. On Monday, the pipes were jointed by a Glasgow squad, who volunteered to complete the job despite a leaking 18-inch gas main nearby. Although the leaking gas joints were covered with wet sacks and the men worked in rotation, one of them was overcome by gas and had to be taken out of the crater. At 7.30 p.m. water was turned on to the 15-inch main and although the water was not declared fit for drinking, John Brown's had a limited supply that night.

Another large water main, one of 12 inches, on Kilbowie Road was badly damaged on Sunday, March 16th, when a large delayed action bomb exploded, causing a crater of about 30 feet wide and 5 feet deep, 8 yards of the water main being displaced and the pipes cracked, and in addition 10 yards of a 6-inch water main being blown out. The next day, a Glasgow squad started on the 12-inch main and a Dumbarton squad on the 6-inch main. It was found impossible to shut off the water in the 12-inch main, the flow never being less than half-pipe. The plans of the piping and connections in the possession of the local Water Trust were unfortunately found to be incorrect, and the failure to shut off the supply to the 12-inch main proved a serious hindrance, additional pumps having to be brought in to enable repairs to proceed. It was not until Wednesday, March 19th, that repairs to the two mains were completed and the water turned on.

Another water main which was seriously damaged in both raids was a 6-inch main in Beardmore Road, Dalmuir. The two bombs fell within 40 yards of each other, destroying the roof over a Glasgow main outfall culvert and forming craters about 30 feet wide and 20 feet deep. In each crater, several yards of the 6-inch main supplying the Royal Ordnance Factory were blown out. On Sunday, March 16th, the Dumbarton Burgh squad started on the repair work and by capping another 6-inch main and closing certain valves provided an alternative feed to the R.O.F. Hardly had this job been completed before a delayed action bomb exploded and again cut off the water supply. The following day a County Council squad took over the repair of the pipes but because of the depth of the crater and the broken length of culvert it was decided to lay a temporary pipe, which was ordered from Messrs. Stavely's stock in Glasgow and supplied within two hours.

Although a water supply was restored as soon as possible, in order to get industrial firms back into production, it was necessary to take precautions against the possibility of contamination: the dosage of chlorination was doubled, notices were ·posted throughout the town and a Ministry of Information loud-speaker van toured the district warning people to boil all water before using. For some time after the water mains had been repaired, the carting of water from Glasgow for drinking and cooking was continued. As the population was much reduced, it was found that three lorries, each with 12 casks of 60 gallons each, were sufficient. Some people in the Whitecrook area thought they could detect a winey flavour in the water from the barrels but it still made good cups of tea. As regards contamination, fears that the damaged sewer on Kilbowie Road might drain into the water supply were finally dispelled by analysis of water samples, carried out by Dr. Mearns of Glasgow University, who showed that the high standard of purity of Clydebank water was maintained. In a report by Department of Health officials who took over control of the repairs on Friday, March 14th, praise was given to McWilliam, the assistant engineer, and Aitkenhead, the foreman, for their courage and resource but there was strong criticism of weaknesses and defects in Clydebank's water supply system. One of the most serious difficulties facing the men on the jobs in Kilbowie Road was the faulty connections of some of the valves, which greatly impeded the repair of the 12-inch main.

'On several occasions, it was found that the information in the water authority's plan was either incorrect or incomplete, which led to a waste of time and labour involved in bringing the wrong materials. In the case of the 12-inch main, which could not be shut off properly, it seems that there is undoubtedly a cross-connection not known to the Water Engineer. In another case, after repairs had been completed, a valve was opened for testing and water rose to the surface round the valve. A further leak was suspected and the street was again opened up. On excavating, it was found that the valve had been put on a branch which was not connected to any other pipe.'

The joints on Clydebank pipes were mainly turned and bored joints which were easily shaken loose by shock and generally a considerable length of pipe had to be taken out on each side of a crack before a sound repair could be made. Difficulties were also experienced through the large number of ball hydrants in the town, which caused wastage of water when pressure was low and retarded the building up of pressure when recharging the mains. The Department advised the replacement of ball hydrants, as occasion arose, by spindle hydrants. From the lengthy list of criticisms in the Department's report, it seems probable that the 'Blitz' had the effect of bringing about much-needed improvements in Clydebank's water supply.

Industrial Production

Reference has been made earlier to the comparatively small amount of damage to industrial establishments, particularly John Brown's shipyard, which was regarded by all, friend and foe, as obviously a primary target. The table published in Appendix C gives details of the actual damage to firms engaged in war production and the extent to which normal production was restored by April 1, 1941. The worst damage occurred in Singer's, where not only was the valuable stock of timber lost but several departments, including the offices, were destroyed or severely damaged. The Royal Ordnance Factory at Dalmuir, which was hit early in the raid (three War Department policemen losing their lives) suffered severe damage and, in addition, production was held up for a time because of damaged water mains. Aitchison Blair at Whitecrook, engaged in the production of small marine engines, was also an early victim of the raids and there was no production for many weeks. Only one firm, the Strathclyde Hosiery Company had its buildings completely destroyed.

The bombing of roads and railways interrupted transport and consequently affected production for some days. Two of the three railway lines, the L.N.E.R. between Dalmuir and Clydebank Central Station, and the L.M.S. at different points between Scotstoun and Dumbarton, were seriously affected by bombs, exploded and unexploded. The route by Clydebank Central Station, which was itself badly damaged, was not opened for a considerable time. John S. Steele, a Depute Head Warden in the A.R.P. service, was awarded the O.B.E. for his courageous leadership during the raids and in particular for his bravery in stopping a passenger train from careering into a bomb crater. Steele had discovered the bomb crater and seeing the train approach he ran towards it, blowing frantically on his whistle and managed to attract the driver's attention. Rothesay Dock, where a puffer was sunk and warehouses destroyed (the stench of burning rubber in one of them hung about the eastern end of Clydebank for days), was not for long out of action and normal river traffic was resumed within a week.

The return to full production was brought about in most firms with remarkable celerity, considering not merely the damage to

installations, machinery and public services but also the difficulties
of the workmen, many of whom had lost their homes and were living
in Rest Centres or in billets miles away from Clydebank. It must be
borne in mind in this connection, however, that a large proportion
of Clydebank firms' work force normally travelled from outside the
burgh, from Glasgow, Dumbarton, the Vale of Leven and even
further afield. An employment return for Thursday, March 20th
showed already a favourable picture, considering that only a few
days had passed since the raids.

	Normal No. Employed	Number Returned
Royal Ordnance Factory	1,681	915
John Brown's	9,917	6,500
Turner's Asbestos Works	260	130
Tullis	450	215
Singer's	No Return	
Aitchison Blair	No contact—works destroyed	

Various measures were taken to encourage the return to work.
Workers were given their meals at the Town Hall until the firms
arranged their own canteens; travel vouchers were supplied free at
first but after the middle of April a maximum payment of 3s. was
required. Whitecrook Primary School was converted by the Scottish
Special Housing Association to accommodate up to 250 homeless
workers.

Before the raids, there had been a widespread strike of Clydeside
apprentice engineers, who felt, with some justification, that their
wages in the last years of apprenticeship, when they were often doing
a journeyman's job, bore little relation to the work they performed.
On Friday, March 14th, after the first raid, the secretary of the
apprentice engineers, John Moore, offered the services of the strikers
to assist in clearing debris, acting as messengers, etc. A Ministry of
Labour Tribunal gave the boys a promise that if they resumed work
their claims would be considered; and the two-weeks-old strike came
to an end on Thursday, March 20th, national negotiations on wages
starting the following day and an award in favour of the apprentices'
claims being made in due course.

Burying the Dead

As might be expected, the heavy casualties in the Clydebank
'Blitz' posed very difficult problems for those responsible for burial
arrangements. In preparation for a possible air raid, a mortuary

Hosiery Mill, Duntocher

Dumbarton Road. Old Kilpatrick

had been set up at the Greyhound Racing Stadium and a large communal grave in the form of a trench had been dug at the cemetery at Dalnottar, the soil being thrown back in but loose enough to be shovelled out again easily. The mortuary, however, was destroyed by a bomb on the first night's raid and emergency mortuaries were established at St. James's Parish Church Hall, at Kilbowie Cemetery and in the new High School building at Janetta Street (which also housed, in another section, an emergency First Aid Post). By Monday, March 17th, many private burials had already been arranged by relatives but there was a large number (about 160) of bodies unclaimed and many of them unidentified. Burials must be conducted normally according to procedures stipulated by law, including the production of a death certificate; and these had to be handled with delicacy and with tact by the officials involved.

By the weekend after the 'Blitz' the Clydebank cemetery employees were busily engaged in private burials arranged by relatives, and a Department of Health official, MacRobbie, came through from Edinburgh on Sunday, March 16th, to supervise the burial of unclaimed bodies. It was decided, in consultation with the District Commissioner, Sir Steven Bilsland, that these should be buried in a communal grave on the following day, Monday the 17th, that Union Jacks should be used as palls, and that the funeral, although not to be publicised, was not to be kept secret. Bilsland made arrangements for Tom Johnston, Secretary of State for Scotland, Sir Iain Colquhoun, Lord Lieutenant of the County, David Kirkwood, M.P., and other notables to attend. MacRobbie managed, with considerable difficulty because of the interruptions in the telephone service, to enlist the aid of Glasgow Corporation, which promised to provide 150 shrouds and the services of 12 grave-diggers, and of Edinburgh Corporation, which promised 9 mortuary attendants. The mass burial at Dalnottar Cemetery was a solemn occasion marred by certain unfortunate but unavoidable features. Because of the restrictions of space in St. James's Church Hall, where undertakers' assistants were also present, engaged in preparing bodies claimed by relatives, the lack of a sufficient number of bearers at the cemetery and of sufficient vans to transport the 67 bodies, delays occurred and the cortege of vans did not leave the hall until a quarter of an hour after the funeral service was due to start. When the first few bodies had been unloaded, Protestant and Catholic clergymen conducted services and wreaths were laid. Thereafter, the official party having left, the rest of the 67 bodies from St. James's Church

Hall were buried. The following day, Tuesday, 33 unclaimed bodies from the school in Janetta Street and 21 from Kilbowie Cemetery were interred.

Sir Steven Bilsland was very angry over the delay in the funeral on Monday afternoon and also over the indecorous manner in which the bodies were wrapped simply in white sheets, with string tied round the waist and neck. But he failed at first to appreciate the tremendous burden placed on those who, without previous experience in many cases, had to discharge a distasteful, if necessary, duty. Clydebank's Sanitary Inspector had actually pressed the Department of Health for a long time before the raids for permission to procure some kind of coffin, even cardboard or papier-mache, but had been refused. When the correspondence was laid before Bilsland, after he had delivered some scathing criticisms of the funeral arrangements, he made full apology to the local officials and turned his wrath on the Department representatives.

Casualty Figures

The question of the number of fatal casualties in Clydebank on March 13-15 was to prove one of the most controversial issues connected with the 'Blitz'. It was not the practice of the Government to publish figures of casualties, as much for reasons of public morale as for reasons of security. But the first statement issued to the press seemed to people on Clydeside to indicate that the Government was attempting, for security and other reasons, to conceal the true facts. The official communique on the raids actually stated that, though the attacks had been heavy, the casualties, though serious, were not expected to be numerous. Such a statement, influenced by the factors mentioned above, was nevertheless based on the incomplete information available at the time, the casualty figures for Clydebank being absent from the first return and only an estimate being included. This communique was followed a few days later, on March 18th, by a statement from the Ministry of Home Security that about 500 persons had been killed in the raids on Clydeside. Actually, a Department of Health report of the same day gave the numbers of those killed, as at 8 p.m. on Sunday, March 16th, as 527 (with a note that to this must probably be added about 200, representing the total of the first raid in Clydebank).

Herbert Morrison, Home Secretary and Minister of Home Security, was challenged by J. McGovern, I.L.P. member for Shettleston, who accused the Minister of making misleading statements and declared that the publication of the figures had caused great resentment on Clydeside. The Solicitor-General, J. S. C. Reid, took the matter up privately with Johnston, Secretary of State for Scotland, referring to the 'frank incredulity' with which Clydebank people had heard the figures broadcast on radio. One Home Guard in Clydebank greeted the report of 500 fatal casualties with the remark, 'Which street?'. It was quite obvious that the Government's statistics were bound to create a feeling of disbelief in official pronouncements generally and also to lead to wildly exaggerated rumours about casualties. Under pressure from newspaper criticism and parliamentary colleagues, Morrison yielded to a certain extent by informing McGovern on April 1st that the total casualties for Clydeside on the two raids were 1,100 killed and 1,000 seriously injured but refused 'for security reasons' to distinguish between Glasgow and Clydebank. In an official (and at that time secret and confidential) report from the Regional Commissioner's office, dated April 3rd, the figures were given as follows:—

	Killed	Seriously Injured
Glasgow	647	390
Clydebank	358	973
Dunbartonshire		
(outside Clydebank)	60	219
Other counties	18	20
TOTAL	1,083	1,620

But the story of the casualty figures was not finished. A year later on the anniversary of the Clydebank 'Blitz', the *Sunday Post* of March 15th, 1942, referred to the 1,200 Clydebank people who lost their lives 'as the result of the savage two-night blitz on the town'. This passage, which had escaped the eagle eyes of the censor, caused a flutter in the dovecotes of St. Andrew's House and other Government offices. Clydebank Town Council debated the whole question of the casualty figures and decided to ask for publication of the official figures 'as exorbitant figures' had been circulating in the burgh but the authorities were still unwilling to do so. The disclosure of the figures for Clydeside as a whole had been made most reluctantly by Herbert Morrison a year before under considerable pressure in order to correct 'injudicious statements' by the Ministry of Home Security soon after the raids. The Town Council returned to the charge and submitted that if the *Sunday Post* figures were incorrect (and many in Clydebank thought they were too low) then a correction should be published. The Ministry, unwilling, as Government departments invariably are, to admit an error and feeling that any further public statement would only reinforce public disquiet about official statistics in general, decided to stand their ground and refused to issue detailed figures. At the time of the Town Council's request, new revised figures were given in a departmental memorandum:

> Total casualties—over 1,200 killed and over 1,100 seriously injured:
> Clydebank—528 killed and 617 seriously injured.

As can be seen from these figures, more were killed outside Clydebank than inside, although this in no way diminishes the gravity of the disaster which befell what had once been called 'the risingest burgh' in Scotland. It may be added that in the list of civilian dead published by the Imperial War Graves Commission in 1954 and printed in Appendix A, the total number of deaths of Clydebank people is only 448.

Curiosities

There are few survivors of the 'Blitz' who have not some curious tales to relate. Many of them relate to the effect of blast—the windscreen of the Wolseley carrying two police officers being sucked out by blast instead of being blown in, when a bomb exploded ahead of the car near Hornbeam Drive; the alarm clock which was blown out of the MacLennans' house in Radnor Street and landed on top of the dustbin; the destruction of everything in the Mannings' house in Young Street except for the dog's dish. At the Callanders' house in Cedar Avenue, the dining table had been set for supper before the raids and was found after the bombs fell to have the legs sticking through the top of the table. Hundreds of old people (and young too, for that matter) left their homes in such a hurry that they forgot to put their dentures in. One such person, rushing to the Anderson shelter in the garden, suddenly paused and then started back to the house. 'Where are you going?' cried his son, 'Back for my teeth,' replied the old one. 'Don't be daft,' said his son. 'It's not pies they're dropping.'

The mornings after the raids produced some curious sights—half a tenement shorn away and a kettle still sitting on a kitchen range; tailors' dummies blown out of a shop window and lying, some of them as if mutilated in macabre fashion, in the middle of the main street; a disconsolate man with an empty bird cage, which had contained a budgerigar and had the door shut before the raid and now, after the raid, was still shut but the bird was gone; a young father heating his baby's milk over the butt-end of an incendiary; and another making tea over a blow-lamp with water taken from a lavatory cistern.

Two stories relate to policemen. Sergeant John MacLeod, who was awarded the George Medal, was in Radnor Street when he heard a bomb come whistling down. He threw himself to the ground to escape the blast and both he and another man beside him were badly shaken. When they rose to their feet, the other man did not seem to be able to talk although he was obviously trying to do so. A week later, MacLeod was boarding a bus when he met the same man face to face. All of a sudden, the man hailed MacLeod and then explained that he had lost his voice as a result of the blast and only regained it at that moment. When the house of Sergeant J. Hutchison at 50 Janetta Street went on fire, the family had no time to save anything. His daughter on her way out seized the first thing which came to her hand and which happened to be her father's helmet. There she stood in the garden looking at the blazing house and then saying, 'What's the sense of saving this when everything else has gone?' and threw the helmet on the flames.

Conclusion

The March raids were not the last on Clydeside. Reference has already been made to the raids of April and May, 1941; but after May the attention of the Germans was directed to their Russian campaign. Only an occasional enemy plane crossed the Scottish coast-line thereafter. The German civilian population was to suffer much heavier bombing than the Luftwaffe ever dreamed of in 1940-41. 'Block-buster' bombs of 10 tons (compared with the heaviest German bomb of 1941, the 'Hermann Goering' of one ton) were used to shatter whole blocks of houses. Hamburg, which is to the Elbe and the north of Germany what Glasgow is to the Clyde and the West of Scotland, was bombarded again and again: between July 24th and July 29th, 1943 there were seven heavy attacks, 2,300 tons of high-explosive bombs being dropped on the latter date. On one night, February 15-16, 1944, Berlin was visited by more than 1,000 British bombers in a display of saturation bombing, 2,500 tons of high-explosives being dropped in 30 minutes.

Some of the names included in the list of Civilian Dead in Clydebank are those of men who died as a result of the 'Blitz' but months afterwards. A parachute mine had fallen into Beardmore's old basin and on September 15th, when tugs were working there, the mine exploded. One of the tugs, the *Atlantic Cock*, had its stern blown off and finished on the other side of the river. The body of one of the tugmen was blown to a terrific height into the air (one observer estimated 70 feet), and in all nine were killed, including the skipper of the tug, A. Stewart of Greenock.

There were others whose deaths resulted at an interval of months or, in some cases, years from the effects of the 'Blitz' and its aftermath. And indeed, even today after more than thirty years, the scars and wounds, physical, mental and spiritual, are still to be found in the persons who lived through the Clydebank 'Blitz'.

Funeral of Unclaimed Victims

Blitz Memorial, Dalnottar Cemetery

LIST OF FATAL CASUALTIES

THE following list of civilian war dead, 1939–1945, was compiled by the Imperial War Graves Commission in 1954 and is to be found in the Roll of Honour placed in Westminster Abbey:

Burgh of Clydebank

ADAMS, MARY, age 55. 14 March 1941, at 3 First Street.

ADAMSON, ARCHIBALD, age 19; Home Guard. Son of John and Mary Adamson, of 4 Rosebery Place. 13 March 1941, at Church Street shelter.

AIRD, ISOBEL, age 18. Daughter of Henry Robert Aird, of 23 Planetree Road, Dalmuir, and of Marion Aird. 13 March 1941, at 10 Church Street.

AIRD, MARION, age 44. Daughter of John Harris, of 5 Cambridge Avenue, and of the late Isabella Harris; wife of Henry Robert Howat Aird, of 23 Planetree Road, Dalmuir. 13 March 1941, at 10 Church Street.

AIRD, TOMINA, age 15. Daughter of Henry Robert Howat Aird, Dalmuir, and of Marion Aird. 13 March 1941, at 10 Church Street.

ANDERSON, ANDREW LAWSON, age 53; of 6 Stanley Street. 15 September 1941, at Beardmore Basin, Dalmuir.

ANDERSON, ESTHER, age 13; of 66 Crown Avenue. Daughter of Thomas Anderson. 14 March 1941, at 66 Crown Avenue.

ANDERSON, GEORGE, age 51; Firewateher; of 20 Kelvingrove Street, Glasgow. Son of the late Alexander Anderson; husband of Alexandria Anderson. 13 March 1941, at Napier Street.

ANDERSON, JOHN CHISHOLM, age 70, of 158A Second Avenue. 13 March 1941, at 158A Second Avenue.

ANDERSON, THOMAS, age 33; of 66 Crown Avenue. 14 March 1941, at 66 Crown Avenue.

BAINBRIDGE, ELLEN NIXON, age 13; of 7 Beardmore Street, Dalmuir. Daughter of Thomas Bainbridge, and of the late Jane Bainbridge. 14 March 1941, at 7 Beardmore Street.

BAINBRIDGE, THOMAS, age 16; of 7 Beardmore Street, Dalmuir. Son of Thomas Bainbridge, and of the late Jane Bainbridge. 14 March 1941, at 7 Beardmore Street.

BAXTER, ELIZABETH COUCH, age 53. Wife of J. Baxter, of 6 Buchanan Street, Dalmuir. 13 March 1941, at 78 Second Avenue.

BEATON, ANNIE, age 10; of Second Avenue. Daughter of James Beaton.

BELL, ROSETTA, age 31. Wife of James G. Bell. 13 March 1941, at 4 Second Terrace.

BENNETT, MARY, age 53. Wife of John Bennett, of 11 Limetree Drive, Parkhall, Dalmuir. 13 March 1941, at 18 Limetree Drive.

BETTY (formerly MIDDLEMISS), ERIC, age 16; of 13 Second Terrace. Adopted son of William and Elizabeth Betty. 15 March 1941 at Clydebank.

BICKER, MARIA, age 73; of 431 Glasgow Road. 13 March 1941, at 431 Glasgow Road.

BLACK, ISABELLA, age 63; of 431 Glasgow Road. Widow of William Francis Black. 13 March 1941, at 431 Glasgow Road.

BLACK, JAMES, age 71; of 431 Glasgow Road. Son of William and Mary Gardiner Black, of 34 Templehill, Troon; husband of Janet Skinner Black. 13 March 1941, at 431 Glasgow Road.

BLYTH, CAROLINE, age 19; of 431 Glasgow Road. Daughter of Robert and Sarah Blyth. 13 March 1941, at 431 Glasgow Road.

BLYTH, ROBERT, age 54; of 431 Glasgow Road. Husband of Sarah Blyth. 13 March 1941, at 431 Glasgow Road.

BLYTH, SARAH, age 54; of 431 Glasgow Road. Wife of Robert Blyth. 13 March 1941, at 431 Glasgow Road.

BORLAND, GEORGINA, age 43; of 57 Whitecrook Street. Daughter of Mr. and Mrs. William Robb, of Holburn Street, Aberdeen; wife of John Peebles Borland. 14 March 1941, at 57 Whitecrook Street.

BORLAND, JESSIE HASLIE age 21 months; of 69 Livingstone Street. Daughter of Hugh Borland (H.M. Forces) and Elizabeth Borland. 13 March 1941, at 69 Livingstone Street.

BORLAND, JOHN PEEBLES, age 44; of 57 Whitecrook Street. Son of Mr. and Mrs. William Borland, of 13 Easwald Bank, Kilbarchan; husband of Georgina Borland. 14 March 1941, at 57 Whitecrook Street.

BOWMAN, ARCHIBALD, age 16; of 10 Church Street. Son of Richard Bowman, and of Lilian May Bowman. 13 March 1941, at 10 Church Street.

BOWMAN, HANNAH, age 19; of 10 Church Street. Daughter of Richard Bowman, and of Lilian May Bowman. 13 March 1941, at 10 Church Street.

BOWMAN, LILIAN MAY, age 46; of 10 Church Street. Wife of Richard Bowman. 13 March 1941, at 10 Church Street.

(For BOWMAN, ALBERT, see Glasgow list).

BOYD, JAMES, age 41. Husband of Elizabeth Boyd, of 433 Dumbarton Road, Dalmuir. 14 March 1941, at 433 Dumbarton Road.

BOYLE, BRIDGET, age 36; of 2 Singer Street. Daughter of Elizabeth Jane Duffy; wife of William Boyle. 13 March 1941, at 74 Second Avenue.

BOYLE, ELIZABETH ANN, age 5; of 2 Singer Street. Daughter of Bridget and William Boyle, 13 March 1941, at 74 Second Avenue.

BOYLE, ISABELLA GILLESPIE, age 10; of 12 Pattison Street, Dalmuir. Daughter of William and Margaret Gow Boyle. 13 March 1941, at 12 Pattison Street.

BOYLE, MARGARET GOW, age 36; of 12 Pattison Street, Dalmuir. Daughter of Isabella Gow, of 126 Second Avenue; wife of William Boyle. 13 March 1941 at 12 Pattison Street.

BOYLE, MARY, age 84; of 78 Jellicoe Street, Dalmuir. 13 March 1941, at 78 Jellicoe Street.

BOYLE, WILLIAM, age 40; of 12 Pattison Street, Dalmuir. Son of William Boyle, of Roman Bridge, Glasgow; husband of Margaret Gow Boyle. 13 March 1941, at 12 Pattison Street.

BOYLE, WILLIAM, age 38; of 2 Singer Street. Son of William and Hannah Boyle, of 24 Delhi Avenue; husband of Bridget Boyle. 13 March 1941, at Second Avenue.

BOYLE, WILLIAM, age 3; of 2 Singer Street. Son of William and Bridget Boyle. 13 March 1941, at 74 Second Avenue.

BRADLEY, CATHERINE HAGGERT, age 24; of 57 Whitecrook Street. Wife of James John Bradley. 14 March 1941, at 57 Whitecrook Street.

BRIMER, JAMES SIMPSON, age 72; of 9 Pattison Street, Dalmuir. Husband of Helen Brimer. 13 March 1941, at 9 Pattison Street.

BUSBY, DANIEL, age 48; of 131 Dumbarton Road; son of Daniel and Mary Busby. 14 March 1941, at 131 Dumbarton Road.

CAHILL, ANNA, age 11; of 72 Second Avenue. Daughter of John Cahill and of Wilhelmina Cahill. 13 March 1941, at 72 Second Avenue.

CAHILL, ELIZABETH, age 10; of 72 Second Avenue. Daughter of John Cahill, and of Wilhelmina Cahill. 13 March 1941, at 72 Second Avenue.

CAHILL, WILHELMINA, age 47; of 72 Second Avenue. Wife of John Cahill. 13 March 1941, at 72 Second Avenue.

CAHILL, WILHELMINA, age 4; of 72 Second Avenue. Daughter of John Cahill, and of Wilhelmina Cahill. 13 March 1941, at 72 Second Avenue.

CAIRNS, MARY, age 50; of 3 Second Terrace. Wife of Thomas Cairns. 13 March 1941, at 3 Second Terrace.

CAMERON, MARGARET, age 16; 13 March 1941, at 78 Jellicoe Street.

CAMPBELL, AGNES, age 22; F.A.P. member; of 14 Broom Drive. Daughter of Archibald Campbell, and of Mary Jane Chambers Campbell. 13 March 1941, at 14 Broom Drive.

CAMPBELL, ALEXANDER, age 39; of 34 Granville Street. 14 March 1941, at 62 Radnor Street.

CAMPBELL, ANNIE, age 16; of 14 Broom Drive. Daughter of Archibald Campbell, and of Mary Jane Chambers Campbell. 13 March 1941, at 14 Broom Drive.

CAMPBELL, DAVID, age 31; of 9 Richard Street, Anderston, Glasgow. Husband of Mary Campbell. 13 March 1941, at Galbraith's Store, Napier Street.

CAMPBELL, ELLEN, age 23; Auxiliary Nurse; of 14 Broom Drive. Daughter of Archibald Campbell, and of Mary Jane Chambers Campbell. 13 March 1941, at 14 Broom Drive.

CAMPBELL, MARTHA, age 21; F.A.P. member; of 14 Broom Drive. Daughter of Archibald Campbell, and of Mary Jane Chambers Campbell. 13 March 1941, at 14 Broom Drive.

CAMPBELL, MARY JANE CHAMBERS, age 52; of 14 Broom Drive. Wife of Archibald Campbell. 13 March 1941, at 14 Broom Drive.

CANNING, ARCHIBALD SMITH, age 3. Son of Archibald Smith Canning and Edith Canning, of 10 Pattison Street, Dalmuir West. 13 March 1941 at 9 Pattison Street.

CANNING, DANIEL, age 2 months. Son of Archibald Smith Canning and Edith Canning, of 10 Pattison Street, Dalmuir West. 13 March 1941, at 9 Pattison Street.

CLARKSON, MARGARET, age 32. Daughter of John O'Donnell, of 53 Clyde Street. 13 March 1941, at Benbow Hotel, Dalmuir.

CLASON, AGNES, age 5. Daughter of John Clason, and of Nellie Clason. 13 March 1941, at 7 Spencer Street.

CLASON, ELIZABETH, age 8. Daughter of John Clason, and of Nellie Clason. 13 March 1941, at 7 Spencer Street.

CLASON, NELLIE, age 31. Wife of John Clason. 13 March 1941, at 7 Spencer Street.

COCHRANE, WALLACE, age 17 months; of 2 Castle Street, Dalmuir. Son of Hugh Cochrane (H.M. Forces). 14 March 1941, at 2 Castle Street.

COGHILL, GEORGE, age 65; of 31 Livingstone Street. 13 March 1941, at 31 Livingstone Street.

COOK, MARY HOPE, age 54. 13 March 1941, at 4 Napier Street.

COOPER, ISABELLA MCLEAN, age 20. Daughter of Mr. and Mrs. Andrew Cooper, of 179 Duntocher Road, Parkhall, Dalmuir. 13 March 1941, at Spencer Street.

COOPER, MINNIE, age 65; of 8 Burn Terrace, Eastfield, Cambuslang, Lanark. Widow of Angus A. Cooper. 13 March 1941, at 12 Beatty Street.

COUTTS, JAMES SMITH, age 37; of 256 Rigby Street, Glasgow. Son of Isabella Coutts, of 46 Planet Street, Glasgow, and of the late Alexander Coutts. 13 March 1941, at Beardmore's Works, Dalmuir.

CRERAND, MICHAEL, age 39. Husband of Sarah Crerand, of 129 Thistle Street, Glasgow. 13 March 1941, at 76B Second Avenue.

CRYAN, JANE, age 74. 13 March 1941, at 9 Pattison Street, Dalmuir.

CULLEN, NORA, age 32. Wife of Patrick Cullen. 13 March 1941, at 74 Second Avenue.

CULLEN, PATRICK, age 27. Son of Alexander Cullen; husband of Nora Cullen. 13 March 1941, at 74 Second Avenue.

CURREN, PATRICK (PETER), age 77; of 10 Spencer Street. Husband of Elizabeth Hopkinson Curran. 13 March 1941, at 10 Spencer Street.

CURRIE, SAMUEL EVANS, age 37; of 12 Beatty Street, Dalmuir. Son of Thomas Lockhead Currie, and of the late Rachel Evans Currie. 13 March 1941, at 12 Beatty Street.

CURRIE, THOMAS LOCKHEAD, age 65; of 12 Beatty Street, Dalmuir. Son of the late Joseph and Agnes Currie, of Paisley; husband of the late Rachel Evans Currie. 13 March 1941, at 12 Beatty Street.

DANIELS, WILLIAM, age 44. Husband of Agnes Daniels. 13 March 1941, at 43 Whin Street.

DEMPSTER, EUPHEMIA, age 54; of 60 Radnor Street. Wife of Gilbert Dempster. 14 March 1941, at 60 Radnor Street.

DEMPSTER, GILBERT, age 54; of 60 Radnor Street. Husband of Euphemia Dempster. 14 March 1941, at 60 Radnor Street.

DEMPSTER, MARY, age 57; of 60 Radnor Street. Widow of Alexander Dempster. 14 March 1941, at 60 Radnor Street.

DEMPSTER, MARY BEST BRADLEY, age 29; of 60 Radnor Street. Daughter of Mary, and of the late Alexander Dempster. 14 March 1941, at 60 Radnor Street.

DENNIS, JEAN, age 59. Wife of Samuel Dennis. 13 March 1941, at 78 Jellicoe Street, Dalmuir.

DENNIS, SAMUEL, age 65. Husband of Jean Dennis. 13 March 1941, at 78 Jellicoe Street, Dalmuir.

DICK, IAN PRENTICE, age 34; A.R.P. Ambulance Driver; of 2A The Crescent, Dalmuir. Son of John Prentice Dick and Elizabeth Ferguson Dick. 14 March 1941, at 2A The Crescent.

DICK, WILLIAM BARR, age 26; of 2A The Crescent, Dalmuir. Son of John Prentice Dick and Elizabeth Ferguson Dick. 14 March 1941, at 2A The Crescent.

DINNING, DUNCAN, age 3; of 2 Castle Street, Dalmuir. Son of David Dinning, and of Jane McPherson Dinning. 14 March 1941, at 2 Castle Street.

DINNING, JANE MCPHERSON, age 41; of 2 Castle Street, Dalmuir. Daughter of Duncan and Janet Hopkirk, of 10 Hutton Drive, South Govan, Glasgow; wife of David Dinning. 14 March 1941, at 2 Castle Street.

DINNING, JANET MITHCELL HOPKIRK, age 15; of 2 Castle Street, Dalmuir. Daughter of David Dinning, and of Jane McPherson Dinning. 14 March 1941, at 2 Castle Street.

DIVER, EDWARD, age 76; of 76 Second Avenue. Son of Hugh and Agnes Diver; husband of Mary Diver. 13 March 1941, at 76 Second Avenue.

DIVER, EDWARD, age 50; of 76 Second Avenue. Son of Edward and Mary Diver. 13 March 1941, at 76 Second Avenue.

DIVER, EDWARD, age 13; of 76 Second Avenue. Son of John Francis and Mary McDermott Diver. 13 March 1941, at 76 Second Avenue.

DIVER, EDWARD, age 8; of 76 Second Avenue. Son of Edward Diver (Junr.) and of the late Mary Dormachie Diver. 13 March 1941, at 76 Second Avenue.

DIVER, HUGH, age 81; of 76 Second Avenue. Husband of the late Catherine McAulay Diver. 13 March 1941, at 76 Second Avenue.

DIVER, JOHN, age 9; of 76 Second Avenue. Son of John Francis and Mary McDermott Diver. 13 March 1941, at 76 Second Avenue.

DIVER, JOHN FRANCIS, age 44; of 76 Second Avenue. Son of Hugh and of the late Catherine McAulay Diver; husband of Mary McDermott Diver. 13 March 1941, at 76 Second Avenue.

DIVER, MARGARET, age 9; of 76 Second Avenue. Daughter of John Francis and Mary McDermott Diver. 13 March 1941, at 76 Second Avenue.

DIVER, MARY, age 76; of 76 Second Avenue. Wife of Edward Diver (Senr.). 13 March 1941, at 76 Second Avenue.

DIVER, MARY MCDERMOTT, age 44; of 76 Second Avenue. Wive of John Francis Diver. 13 March 1941, at 76 Second Avenue.

DIVERS, ADAM, age 11; of 431 Glasgow Road. Son of James and Margaret Anderson Divers. 13 March 1941, at 431 Glasgow Road.

DIVERS, JAMES, age 54; of 431 Glasgow Road. Son of Mr. and Mrs. James Divers; husband of Margaret Anderson Divers. 13 March 1941, at 431 Glasgow Road.

DIVERS, JAMES, age 17; of 431 Glasgow Road. Son of James and Margaret Anderson Divers. 13 March 1941, at 431 Glasgow Road.

DIVERS, MARGARET ANDERSON, age 46; of 431 Glasgow Road. Daughter of Mr. and Mrs. Chalmers, of Miller Street, Larkhall; wife of James Divers. 13 March 1941, at 431 Glasgow Road.

DOCHERTY, ROSE, age 15; 13 March 1941, at 4 Napier Street.

DOHERTY, EVELYN, age 6; of 2 Napier Street. Daughter of Nancy Doherty, and of Francis Doherty. 13 March 1941, at 2 Napier Street.

DOHERTY, FRANCIS, age 43; of 2 Napier Street. Husband of Nancy Doherty. 13 March 1941, at 2 Napier Street.

DOHERTY, FRANCIS JOSEPH, age 15; of 2 Napier Street. Son of Nancy Doherty, and of Francis Doherty. 13 March 1941, at 2 Napier Street.

DOHERTY, JOHN ANTHONY, age 13; of 2 Napier Street. Son of Nancy Doherty, and of Francis Doherty. 13 March 1941, at 2 Napier Street.

DOHERTY, MARGARET (RITA), age 10; of 2 Napier Street. Daughter of Nancy Doherty, and of Francis Doherty. 13 March 1941, at 2 Napier Street.

DOHERTY, MARY, age 19; of 2 Napier Street. Daughter of Nancy Doherty, and of Francis Doherty. 13 March 1941, at 2 Napier Street.

DOLAN, MARY, age 15; of 66 Crown Avenue. Daughter of Mary Dolan, and of Thomas Dolan. 14 March 1941, at 66 Crown Avenue.

DOLAN, THOMAS, age 49; of 66 Crown Avenue. Husband of Mary Dolan. 14 March 1941, at 66 Crown Avenue.

(For DOLAN, THOMAS PAUL, see Glasgow list)

DONALDSON, EDWARD WILLIAM MOWAT, age 47; Air Raid Warden; of 31 Livingstone Street. Husband of Catherine Donaldson. 13 March, 1941, at 31 Livingstone Street.

DONNELLY, HUGH, age 11; of 7 Pattison Street, Dalmuir. Son of Mary Catherine, and of the late Francis Donnelly. 13 March 1941, at 7 Pattison Street.

DONNELLY, MARGARET, age 6; of 7 Pattison Street, Dalmuir. Daughter of Mary Catherine, and of the late Francis Donelly. 13 March 1941, at 7 Pattison Street.

DONNELLY, MARY CATHERINE, age 42; of 7 Pattison Street, Dalmuir. Widow of Francis Donnelly. 13 March 1941, at 7 Pattison Street.

DONNELLY, MAUREEN, age 8; of 7 Pattison Street, Dalmuir. Daughter of Mary Catherine, and of the late Francis Donnelly. 13 March 1941, at 7 Pattison Street.

DONNELLY, ROSELEEN, age 14; of 7 Pattison Street, Dalmuir. Daughter of Mary Catherine, and of the late Francis Donnelly. 13 March 1941, at 7 Pattison Street.

DONNELLY, THERESA, age 4; of 7 Pattison Street, Dalmuir. Daughter of Mary Catherine, and of the late Francis Donelly. 13 March 1941, at 7 Pattison Street.

DORAN, CHARLES, age 62; of 74 Second Avenue. Husband of Mary Doran. 13 March 1941, at 74 Second Avenue.

DORAN, ISABELLA, age 25; of 74 Second Avenue. Daughter of Charles and Mary Doran. 13 March 1941, at 74 Second Avenue.

DORAN, MARY, age 65; of 74 Second Avenue. Wife of Charles Doran. 13 March 1941, at 74 Second Avenue.

DRUMMOND, GLADYS, age 38; of 12 Pattison Street, Dalmuir. Wife of Ralph Andrew Drummond. 13 March 1941, as 12 Pattison Street.

DRUMMOND, JAMES CARRIGAN, age 7; of 12 Pattison Street, Dalmuir. Son of Ralph Andrew and Gladys Drummond. 13 March 1941, at 12 Pattison Street.

DRUMMOND, RALPH ANDREW, age 40; of 12 Pattison Street, Dalmuir. Husband of Gladys Drummond. 13 March 1941, at 12 Pattison Street.

DRUMMOND, RALPH ANDREW, age 10; of 12 Pattison Street, Dalmuir. Son of Ralph Andrew and Gladys Drummond. 13 March 1941, at 12 Pattison Street.

DUFFY, ELIZABETH JANE, age 64; of 74 Second Avenue. 13 March 1941, at 74 Second Avenue.

DUNCAN, THOMAS, age 90 Son of Julia Duncan. 13 March 1941, at 27 Graham Avenue.

DUNCAN, WILLIAM WHITE, age 37; of 64 Crown Avenue. Son of the late John Duncan, of Broomlands Cottage, Irvine. 14 March 1941, at 64 Crown Avenue.

DUNLEAVY, JAMES, age 54; of Benbow Hotel, Dalmuir. 13 March 1941, at Janetta Street.

DUNN, ANDREW, age 62; of 131 Dumbarton Road. Son of John and Mary Campbell Dunn, of Old Kirkpatrick; husband of Mary Busby Dunn. 14 March 1941, at 131 Dumbarton Road.

DUNN, GRACE, age 43; of 72 Second Avenue. Wife of John Dunn. 14 March 1941, at 59 Whitecrook Street.

DUNN, GRACE, age 20; Nurse; of 72 Second Avenue. 13 March 1941, at 74 Second Avenue.

DUNN, JOHN, age 24; of 131 Dumbarton Road. Son of Mary Busby Dunn, and of Andrew Dunn. 14 March 1941, at 131 Dumbarton Road.

DUNN, MARY, age 42; of 72 Second Avenue. 13 March 1941, at 74 Second Avenue.

DUNN, MARY MARTIN, age 38; of 131 Dumbarton Road. Daughter of Mary Busby Dunn, and of Andrew Dunn. 14 March 1941, at 131 Dumbarton Road.

FINDLAY, JAMES SUMMERS, age 13 months; of 159 Second Avenue. Son of Findlay, and of John Duthie Findlay. 13 March 1941, at Second Avenue.

FINDLAY, JOHN DUTHIE, age 26; of 159 Second Avenue. Son of Mrs. E. Findlay, of 13 Singer Street; husband of C. Findlay. 13 March 1941, at Second Avenue.

FINNEN, CHARLES, age 16 months; of 31 Graham Avenue. Son of Mr. and Mrs. James Finnen. 13 March 1941, at Second Avenue.

FLEMMING, JOHN, age 24; of 41 Whin Street, North Kilbowie. Son of James and Annie Flemming. 13 March 1941, at Whin Street.

FORRESTER, JOHN, age 57; of 1 Spencer Street. 13 March 1941, at 1 Spencer Street.

FORRESTER, MARGARET, age 48; of 1 Spencer Street. 13 March 1941, at 1 Spencer Street.

FOTHERINGHAM, CHRISTINA, age 72; of 775 Dumbarton Road, Dalmuir. 14 March 1941, at 775 Dumbarton Road.

FRANCE, JANET, age 54; of 57 Whitecrook Street. Widow of Archibald France, 14 March 1941, at 57 Whitecrook Street.

FRASER, MARGARET, age 42; of 12 Pattison Street. Wife of Alexander Fraser. 13 March 1941, at 57 Whitecrook Sgreet.

FURMAGE, JOHN, age 33; Son of George and Margaret Low Furmage, of 162 Thistle Street, Camelon, Falkirk; husband of Margaret Furmage, of 16A Bute Street, Falkirk. 14 March 1941, at 57 Whitecrook Street.

GALLACHER, DELIA, age 15. 13 March 1941, at 10 Pattison Street.

GALLACHER, MARGARET TERESA DONAGHUE, age 30; of 8 East Barns Street. 13 March 1941, at 2 Napier Street.

GALLAGHER, THOMAS, age 13; of 74 John Knox Street. Son of Thomas and Mary Gallagher. 13 March 1941, at 2 Napier Street.

GALLOWAY, THOMAS THOMSON, age 22; of 57 Whitecrook Street. Son of James Galloway, and of Martha Thomson Galloway. 14 March 1941, at 57 Whitecrook Street.

(For GALLOWAY, MARTHA THOMSON, see Glasgow list).

GEDDES (otherwise THOMSON), WILLIAM, age 15; of 57 Whitecrook Street. Son of Helen Wade (formerly Geddes). 14 March 1941, at 57 Whitecrook Street. (His sister Jessie Chalmers Wade was also killed in the same incident.)

GIBSON, JOHN YOUNG, age 54; of 6 Whin Street. Son of the late James and Margaret Neish Gibson; husband of Mary Rae Gibson. 13 March 1941, at Whin Street.

GILLIES, ANNIE, age 62; of 76 Second Avenue. 13 March 1941, at Second Avenue.

GILLIES, MARGARET MCLAREN, age 23; of 76 Second Avenue. Daughter of Annie Gillies. 13 March 1941, at Second Avenue.

GIVEN, ELIZABETH, age 30; of 57 Whitecrook Street. Daughter of Mr. and Mrs. W. J. Reid, of 432 Dumbarton Road, Dalmuir; wife of William Given. 14 March 1941, at 57 Whitecrook Street.

GRAHAM, ARCHIBALD, age 41. A.R.P. Rescue Service; of 161 Second Avenue. Son of the late Charles and Mary Ann Graham. 13 March 1941, at 161 Second Avenue.

GRAHAM, ANDREW, age 67; of 4 Rosebery Place. 13 March 1941, at Glasgow Road.

GRAHAM, PETER, age 52; husband of Cecilia Graham, of 12 Cherry Crescent. 13 March 1941, at Wardens' Post, Janetta Street.

GRAY, JOHN, age 69. 14 March 1941, at 39 John Knox Street.

GUINEY, MADGE, age 16; of 6 Second Avenue. Daughter of Jack Guiney, of Dromore, Co. Down, Northern Ireland, and of Sarah Guiney. 15 March 1941, at 78 Clarence Street.

GUINEY, SARAH, age 45; of 6 Second Avenue. Daughter of Sam McKee, of Dromore, Co. Down, Northern Ireland; wife of Jack Guiney. 15 March 1941, at 78 Clarence Street.

HAGGARTY, ROBERT JAMES, age 7; of 425 Glasgow Road. Son of Catherine Haggarty, 13 March 1941, at 425 Glasgow Road.

HAMILTON, THOMAS MCLAUGHLIN, age 37; of 69 Livingstone Street. Husband of Jessie Hamilton. 13 March 1941, at 69 Livingstone Street.

HARRIS, SAMUEL, age 69; of 72 Second Avenue, Radnor Park. Husband of the late Sarah Arton Harris. 13 March 1941, at 72 Second Avenue.

HART, HUGH, age 60; of 51 Radnor Street. 14 March 1941, at 72 Second Avenue.

HARVEY, JAMES, age 13; of 25 Graham Avenue. Son of James and Catherine Harvey. 13 March 1941, at 25 Graham Avenue.

HEGGIE, CHARLOTTE, age 10; of 66 Crown Avenue. Daughter of William Heggie, and of Elizabeth Heggie. 14 March 1941, at 66 Crown Avenue

HEGGIE, ELIZABETH, age 32; of 66 Crown Avenue. Daughter of Mr. and Mrs. Abbott; wife of William Heggie. 14 March 1941, at 66 Crown Avenue.

HENDERSON, GEORGE, age 48; of 8 Rowan Drive, Parkhall, Dalmuir. 13 March 1941, at 8 Rowan Drive.

(*For* HENDERSON, JOHN GREEN, *see Dumbarton list*).

HENDERSON, MARY, age 41; of 2 Napier Street. Wife of John Henderson. 13 March 1941, at 2 Napier Street.

HENRY, CHARLES, age 74; of 163 Second Avenue. Husband of Elizabeth Henry. 13 March 1941, at 163 Second Avenue.

HENRY, ELIZABETH, age 65; of 163 Second Avenue. Wife of Charles Henry. 13 March 1941, at 163 Second Avenue.

HISLOP, GEORGE ALEXANDER, age 65; of 672 Dumbarton Road, Dalmuir. Son of the late David and Mary Ann Hislop; husband of Marthesa Maria Hislop. 14 March 1941, at 672 Dumbarton Road.

HISLOP, MARTHESA MARIA, age 65; of 672 Dumbarton Road, Dalmuir. Daughter of the late Alexander and Isabella Ross Hay, of 9 Crichton Street, Edinburgh; wife of George Alexander Hislop. 14 March 1941, at 672 Dumbarton Road.

HOWIE, ALEXANDER, age 19; of 89 Dumbarton Road. Son of George Robert Duncan Howie, and Agnes Millar Howie. 14 March 1941, at The Crescent, Dalmuir.

HOWIE, JANE GILLIAN, age 24; B.R.C.S.; of 89 Dumbarton Road. Daughter of George Robert Duncan Howie, and Agnes Millar Howie. 14 March 1941, at The Crescent Dalmuir.

HUGHES, CATHERINE MCLACHLAN, age 59; of 14 Greer Quadrant, Radnor Park. Wife of David Henry Hughes. 13 March 1941, at 14 Greer Quadrant.

HUGHES, CHARLES, age 61; 13 March 1941, at 18 Broom Drive.

HUGHES, MICHAEL, age 72; of 2 Napier Street. Son of Michael and Catherine Hughes; husband of Sarah Jane Hughes, 13 March 1941, at 2 Napier Street

HUGHES, SARAH JANE, age 68; of 2 Napier Street. Daughter of James and Emma Boyd; wife of Michael Hughes. 13 March 1941, at 2 Napier Street.

HUNTER, MARY ASTON, age 16. Daughter of A. Hunter, and of Sarah Aston Hunter. 13 March 1941, at 19 Beech Drive.

HUNTER, SARAH ASTON, age 43. Wife of A. Hunter. 13 March 1941, at 19 Beech Drive.

HUNTER, WILLIAM SOMERVILLE, age 49; of Kenilworth, Albert Road. Husband of Elizabeth Thomson Hunter. 13 March 1941, at 76 Second Avenue.

JOBLING, DANIEL, age 9. Son of Mary Jobling. 13 March 1941, at 74 Second Avenue.

JOBLING, JAMES, age 11. Son of Mary Jobling. 13 March 1941, at 74 Second Avenue.

JOBLING, JOHN, age 16. Son of Mary Jobling. 13 March 1941, at 74 Second Avenue.

JOBLING, MARY, age 39. 13 March 1941, at 74 Second Avenue.

JOBLING, WILLIAM, age 17. Son of Mary Jobling. 13 March 1941, at 74 Second Avenue.

JOHNSTON, ANNIE HARRIS, age 54; of 2 Castle Street, Dalmuir. Daughter of the late Alexander and Annie Harris Morrison, of 714 Springfield Road, Glasgow; widow of James Johnston. 14 March 1941, at 2 Castle Street.

JOHNSTONE, PETER HUNTER, age 44; Police Sgt., War Department; 9 Golf View Drive, Dalmuir. Son of the late George and Helen Hunter Johnstone, of 25 Trend Hill Green; husband of Thomasina Aird Johnstone. 13 March 1941, at Ordnance Factory, Dalmuir.

KELLY, DORIS, age 16. Daughter of Hugh and Sarah Kelly. 14 March 1941, at 60 Radnor Street.

KELLY, HUGH, age 49. Husband of Sarah Kelly. 14 March 1941, at 60 Radnor Street.

KELLY, JAMES, age 2; of 8 Pattison Street, Dalmuir. Son of Edward Kelly, and of Mary Kelly. 13 March 1941, at 9 Pattison Street.

KELLY, MARY, age 31; of 8 Pattison Street, Dalmuir. Wife of Edward Kelly. 13 March 1941, at 9 Pattison Street.

KELLY, SARAH, age 47. Wife of Hugh Kelly. 14 March 1941, at 60 Radnor Street.

KENNEDY, ELLEN, age 20; of 24 Jellicoe Street, Dalmuir. Daughter of Charles and Mary McQuade Kerr, of 85 College Street; wife of Hugh Alexander Kennedy. 13 March 1941, at 9 Pattison Street.

KENNEDY, HUGH ALEXANDER, age 23; of 24 Jellicoe Street, Dalmuir. Son of Mary Kennedy; husband of Ellen Kennedy. 13 March 1941, at 9 Pattison Street.

KERNACHAN, ANNIE MCKIE, age 8. Daughter of Janet Kernachan. 13 March 1941, at 78 Jellicoe Street.

KERNACHAN, JANET, age 41. 13 March 1941, at 78 Jellicoe Street.

KERNACHAN, RICHARD, age 45; of 78 Jellicoe Street. 14 March 1941, at Castle Street.

KIDD, JEAN (JEANNIE BLACK), age 13; of 57 Abbott Crescent. Daughter of Jessie Kidd. 13 March 1941, at 425 Glasgow Road.

KILPATRICK, AGNES LOCHHEAD, age 31; of 12 Beatty Street, Dalmuir. Wife of Andrew David M. Kilpatrick. 13 March 1941, at 12 Beatty Street.

KILPATRICK, ANDREW DAVID M., age 31; of 12 Beatty Street, Dalmuir. Husband of Agnes Lochhead Kilpatrick. 13 March 1941, at 12 Beatty Street.

KING, HELEN, age 67; of 16 Alder Road, Parkhall, Dalmuir. Widow of Joseph King. 13 March 1941, at 16 Alder Street.

(*For* KING, ROBERT, *see Stirling list*).

LAWRIE, JAMES, age 26; of 57 Whitecrook Street. Son of Archibald and Christina Lawrie. 14 March 1941, at 57 Whitecrook Street.

LECKIE, JAMES, age 73; of 34 Granville Street. 14 March 1941, at Granville Street.

LEE, EVELYN, age 7; of 163 Second Avenue. Daughter of James Lee, and of Margaret Mary Lee. 13 March 1941, at Wardens' Post, Janetta Street.

LEE, JAMES, age 5; of 163 Second Avenue. Son of James Lee, and of Margaret Mary Lee. 13 March 1941, at Wardens' Post, Janetta Street.

LEE, KATHLEEN, age 9; of 163 Second Avenue. Daughter of James Lee, and of Margaret Mary Lee. 13 March 1941, at Wardens' Post, Janetta Street.

LEE, MARGARET, age 11; of 163 Second Avenue. Daughter of James Lee, and of Margaret Mary Lee. 13 March 1941, at Wardens' Post, Janetta Street.

LEE, MARGARET MARY, age 32; of 163 Second Avenue. Daughter of Mr. and Mrs. Michael McNally, of Austin Friars, Mullingar, Co. Westmeath, Irish Republic; wife of James Lee. 13 March 1941, at Wardens' Post, Janetta Street.

LINDSAY, JOHN, age 10. Son of D. Lindsay, and of Violet Lindsay. 13 March 1941, at 74 Second Avenue.

LINDSAY, MARGARET, age 7. Daughter of D. Lindsay, and of Violet Lindsay, 13 March 1941, at 74 Second Avenue.

LINDSAY, VIOLET, age 40. Wife of D. Lindsay. 13 March 1941, at Second Avenue.

LOCHHEAD, ALEXANDER, age 17; Firewatcher. Son of Robert and Martha Lochhead, of 13 Gordon Street. 14 March 1941, at 62 Radnor Street.

LOCKWOOD, ELIZABETH, age 14; of 60 Radnor Street. Daughter of James Lockwood, and of Margaret Sanders Lockwood. 14 March 1941, at 60 Radnor Street.

LOCKWOOD, FREDERICK, age 10; of 60 Radnor Street. Son of James Lockwood, and of Margaret Sanders Lockwood. 14 March 1941, at 60 Radnor Street.

LOCKWOOD, MARGARET, age 5; of 60 Radnor Street. Daughter of James Lockwood and of Margaret Sanders Lockwood. 14 March 1941, at 60 Radnor Street.

LOCKWOOD, MARGARET SANDERS, age 38; of 60 Radnor Street. Daughter of Andrew Sanders; wife of James Lockwood. 14 March 1941, at 60 Radnor Street.

LOGAN, JOSEPH, age 24; of 8 Wallace Street. Son of Letitia Logan, and of, the late William Logan. 13 March 1941, at 76B Second Avenue.

LOUGHLIN, MARY, age 19; daughter of Michael and Ellen Loughlin, of 45 Erskine View, Old Kilpatrick. 13 March 1941, at Jellicoe Street, Dalmuir.

LYONS, WILLIAM ROBERT, age 52; Sgt., Police War Reserve. Hubsand of M. E. Lyons, of 17 Blythswood Drive, Paisley, Renfrewshire. 13 13 March 1941, at Royal Ordnance Factory, Dalmuir.

MCAULAY, JOSEPHINE, age 9; of 7 Beardmore Street, Dalmuir. Daughter of James and Margaret McAulay. 14 March 1941, at 7 Beardmore Street.

MCBRIDE, JOSEPH, age 38; of 431 Glasgow Road. 13 March 1941, at 431 Glasgow Road.

MCCLELLAND, MARINA, age 4. Daughter of J. McClelland, and of Marion McClelland. 13 March 1941, at 431 Glasgow Road.

MCCLELLAND, MARION, age 32; daughter of Maria Bicker. Wife of J. McClelland. 13 March 1941, at 431 Glasgow Road.

MCCLORY, ANNIE, age 9; of 7 Beardmore Street, Dalmuir. Daughter of Matthew McClory, R.N., and of Sara McClory. 14 March 1941, at 7 Beardmore Street.

MCCLORY, JAMES, age 7; of 7 Beardmore Street, Dalmuir. Son of Matthew McClory, R.N., and of Sarah McClory. 14 March 1941, at 7 Beardmore Street.

MCCLORY, JOHN, age 5; of 7 Beardmore Street, Dalmuir. Son of Matthew McClory, R.N., and of Sarah McClory. 14 March 1941, at 7 Beardmore Street.

MCCLORY, MARY, age 3; of 7 Beardmore Street, Dalmuir. Daughter of Matthew McClory, R.N., and of Sarah McClory. 14 March 1941, at 7 Beardmore Street.

MCCLORY, MATTHEW, age 10; of 7 Beardmore Street, Dalmuir. Son of Matthew McClory, R.N., and of Sarah McClory. 14 March 1941, at 7 Beardmore Street.

MCCLORY, SARAH, age 36; of 7 Beardmore Street, Dalmuir. Wife of Matthew McClory, R.N., 14 March 1941, at 7 Beardmore Street.

MCCONNELL, HUGH, age 20; of 2 Napier Street. Son of William McConnell, and of Mary Kate McConnell. 13 March 1941, at 2 Napier Street.

MCCONNELL, MARY FRANCIS, age 21; of 2 Napier Street. Daughter of William McConnell, and of Mary Kate McConnell. 13 March 1941, at 2 Napier Street.

MCCONNELL, MARY KATE, age 39; of 2 Napier Street. Wife of William McConnell. 13 March 1941, at 2 Napier Street.

MCCORMACK, JAMES, age 19; of 54 Jellicoe Street, Dalmuir. Son of John and Sarah McCormack. 13 March 1941, at Jellicoe Street.

MCDONALD, BRENDA, age 5; of 7 Pattison Street, Dalmuir. Daughter of James McDonald, and of Christina McDonald. 13 March 1941, at 7 Pattison Street.

MCDONALD, CHRISTINA, age 36; of 7 Pattison Street, Dalmuir. Daughter of Mrs. MacNair, of 263 Glasgow Road; wife of James McDonald, 13 March 1941,. 7 Pattison Street.

MCDONALD, JAMES, age 10; of 7 Pattison Street, Dalmuir. Son of James McDonald, and of Christina McDonald. 13 March 1941, at 7 Pattison Street.

MCDONALD, JESSIE GRIBBON, age 16; of 7 Pattison Street, Dalmuir. Daughter of James McDonald, and of Christina McDonald. 13 March 1941, at 7 Pattison Street.

MCDONALD, JOHN, age about 65; of 31 Cornock Street. 13 Mrach 1941, at Janetta Street.

MCDOUGALL, MALCOLM GEORGE H., age 70. 13 March 1941, at 72 Jellicoe Street, Dalmuir.

MCFADDEN, MARGARET, age 31; of 2 Napier Street. Daughter of Thomas John McFadden. 13 March 1941, at 2 Napier Street. ˙

MCFADDEN, MICHAEL, age 50. 13 March 1941, at 2 Napier Street.

MCFADDEN, THOMAS JOHN, age 52; of 2 Napier Street. 15 March 1941, at Robroyston Hospital, Glasgow.

MACFARLANE, ROBERT MELONE, age 18; A.R.P. Messenger; of 9 Hill Street. Son of Robert and Margaret I. Macfarlane. 13 March 1941, at Broom Drive.

MCGEADY, PATRICK, age 65; of 18 Miller Street. 13 March 1941, at 11 Second Avenue.

MCGEEHAN, JOHN ANTHONY, age 13; of 781 Dumbarton Road, Dalmuir. Son of John J. and Alice M. F. F. McGeehan. 14 March 1941, at 871 Dumbarton Road.

MCGILL, JOHN, age 10; of 76 Second Avenue. Son of John McGill, and of Mary McGill. 13 March 1941, at 76 Second Avenue.

MGGILL, MARY, age 47; of 76 Second Avenue. Daughter of Edward and Mary Diver; wife of John McGill. 13 March 1941, at 76 Second Avenue.

MACGREGOR, AGNES HUNTER, age 55; of 9 Pattison Street, Dalmuir. Widow of John MacGregor. 14 March 1941, at 9 Pattison Street.

MCGUIGAN, KATHLEEN, age 15; of 4 Napier Street. Daughter of John McGuigan, and of Theresa McGuigan. 13 March 1941, at 4 Napier Street.

MCGUIGAN, THERESA, age 44; of 4 Napier Street. Wife of John McGuigan. 13 March 1941, at 4 Napier Street.

MCINTYRE, AGNES MCLEAN GRAHAM, age 59; of 431 Glasgow Road. Daughter of the later Charles Graham, of 5 Campbell Street; widow of James Grant McIntyre. 13 March 1941, at 431 Glagow Road.

MACK, GEORGE, age 18; of 6 Hornbeam Drive, Parkhall, Dalmuir. Son of Elizabeth Mack, and of John Mack. 14 March 1941, at 6 Hornbeam Drive.

MACK, JAMES, age 35; of 6 Hornbeam Drive, Parkhall, Dalmuir. Son of Elizabeth Mack, and of John Mack. 14 March 1941, at 6 Hornbeam Drive.

MACK, JOHN, age 64; M.M.; of 6 Hornbeam Drive Parkhall, Dalmuir. Husband of Elizabeth Mack. 14 March 1941, at 6 Hornbeam Drive.

McKAIN, JANE, age 39; of 21 Bannerman Street. 13 March 1941, at 425 Glasgow Road.

McKAIN, JEANIE BLACK, age 56; of 57 Abbott Crescent. 13 March 1941, at 425 Glasgow Road.

McKAY, AGNES, age 22; of 35 Graham Avenue, Radnor Park. Daughter of Mr. and Mrs. Charles Dempster, of the the same address; wife of William McKay. 13 March 1941, at 161 Second Avenue.

McKECHNIE, AGNES, age 34; of 12 Pattison Street, Dalmuir. Wife of Michael John Sidney McKechnie. 13 March 1941, at 12 Pattison Street.

McKECHNIE, EMMA SHEILA, age 9; of 12 Pattison Street, Dalmuir. Daughter of Michael John Sidney and Agnes McKechnie. 13 March 1941, at 12 Pattison Street.

McKECHNIE, MICHAEL JOHN SIDNEY, age 34; of 12 Pattison Street, Dalmuir. Son of Michael and Sarah McKechnie, of 65 West Clyde Street, Helensburgh; husband of Agnes McKechnie, 13 March 1941, at 12 Pattison Street.

McKECHNIE, WILLIAM, age 39; of 1 Elm Road, Dalmuir. 13 March 1941, at 425 Glasgow Road.

McKENDRICK, MARGARET, age 6. Daughter of Robert McKendrick. 13 March 1941, at 4 Napier Street.

McKENDRICK, ROBERT, age 4. Son of Robert McKendrick. 13 March 1941, at 4 Napier Street.

McKENDRICK, THOMAS, age 8. Son of Robert McKendrick. 13 March 1941, at 4 Napier Street.

McKENZIE, ALEXANDER, age 70; of 78 Second Avenue, Radnor Park. Husband of the late Margaret Beadie McKenzie. 13 March 1941, at 78 Second Avenue.

McKENZIE, ANGUS, age 32; of 425 Glasgow Road. Husband of Martha McKenzie. 13 March 1941, at 425 Glasgow Road.

McKENZIE, JOHN, age 56; of 76 Second Avenue. Son of Alexander, and of the late Margaret Beadie McKenzie; husband of Mary McKenzie. 13 March 1941, at 76 Second Avenue.

McKENZIE, MARGARET, age 16; of 66 Crown Avenue. Daughter of Mr. J. McKenzie. 21 March 1941, at 64 Crown Avenue.

McKENZIE, MARTHA, age 36; of 425 Glasgow Road. Wife of Angus McKenzie. 13 March 1941, at 425 Glasgow Road.

McKENZIE, MARY, age 59; of 76 Second Avenue. Daughter of the late Alexander and Elizabeth Hannah; wife of John McKenzie. 13 March 1941, at Second Avenue.

MACKENZIE, MURDOCH, age 56; of 39 Old Dumbarton Road, Glasgow. 13 March 1941, at Ordnance Factory, Dalmuir.

McKENZIE ROBERT McEWAN, age 3; of 425 Glasgow Road. Son of Angus and Martha McKenzie. 13 March 1941, at 425 Glasgow Road.

McKINLAY, JOHN, age 30; Air Raid Warden; of 425 Glasgow Road. Son of Catherine McKinlay, of 3 Kitchener Street, Dalmuir, and of William McKinlay; husband of Marion McKain McKinlay; 13 13 March 1941, at 425 Glasgow Road.

McKINLAY, MARION McKAIN, age 27; of 425 Glasgow Road. Daughter of Mr. and Mrs. R. McKain, of 57 Abbott Crescent; wife of John McKinlay. 13 March 1941, at 425 Glasgow Road.

McKINLAY, WILLIAM, age 64; of 3 Kitchener Street. Husband of Catherine McKinlay. 13 March 1941, at 76 Second Avenue.

McKINLAY, WILLIAM FERGUSON, age 6; of 425 Glasgow Road. Son of John and Marion McKain McKinlay. 13 March 1941, at 425 Glasgow Road.

McLAFFERTY, JOHN, age 46; of 15 Livingstone Street. 13 March 1941, at La Scala Picture House.

McLEAN, DAVID McCOURT, age 17; of 78 Jellicoe Street, Dalmuir. Son of John and Edith Mark McLean. 13 March 1941, at 78 Jellicoe Street.

McLEAN, EDITH MARK, age 47; of 78 Jellicoe Street, Dalmuir. Daughter of Alexander and Margaret Craig; wife of John McLean. 13 March 1941, at 78 Jellicoe Street.

McLEAN, JAMES GIVEN SPENCE, age 13; of 78 Jellicoe Street, Dalmuir. Son of John and Edith Mark McLean. 13 March 1941, at 78 Jellicoe Street.

McLEAN, JEANIE ELLIOTT, age 47; of 4 Cherry Crescent, North Kilbowie. Wife of Dugald McLean. 13 March 1941, at Wardens' Post, Janetta Street.

McLEAN, JOHN, age 56; of 78 Jellicoe Street, Dalmuir. Son of John and Catherine McLean; husband of Edith Mark McLean. 13 March 1941, at 78 Jellicoe Street.

McLEAN, MARGARET, age 18; of 4 Cherry Crescent, North Kilbowie. Daughter of Dugald McLean, and of Jeanie Elliott McLean. 13 March 1941, at Wardens' Post, Janetta Street.

McLENNAN, ALEXANDER BLAIR, age 65; of Benbow Hotel, Dalmuir. Son of James and Janet McLennan, of 27 Durcene Street, Stirling. 13 March 1941, at Benbow Hotel.

McLENNAN, NORMAN, age 7; of 9 Pattison Street, Dalmuir. Son of the late Norman McLennan. 13 March 1941, at 9 Pattison Street.

McMILLAN, EDWARD, age 15; of 7 Pattison Street, Dalmuir. Son of David and Elizabeth McMillan. 13 March 1941, at Pattison Street.

McMORROW, PATRICK, age 65; of 12 Pattison Street, Dalmuir. Husband of Sarah McMorrow. 13 March 1941, at 12 Pattison Street.

McMORROW, SARAH, age 56; of 12 Pattison Street, Dalmuir. Daughter of the late Charles and Grace McGroarty, of Drumnavough, Glendwan, Co. Donegal, Irish Republic; wife of Patrick McMorrow. 13 March 1941, at 12 Pattison Street.

McNAMARA, DAVID, 13 March 1941, at Benbow Hotel, Dalmuir.

McPHERSON, JANET RICHARDSON, age 38; wife of William McPherson, of 3 Somerville Terrace, Bowling. 13 March 1941, at Pattison Street, Dalmuir.

McRae, Alexander, age 83; of 32 Park Road, Dalmuir. Husband of Catherine A. McRae. 14 March 1941, at 32 Park Road.

McSherry, Edward, age 12; of 161 Second Avenue. Son of Mary Jane, and of the late Matthew McSherry. 13 March 1941, at 161 Second Avenue.

McSherry, James Andrew, age 10 months; of 161 Second Avenue. Son of Mary Jane, and of the late Matthew McSherry. 13 March 1941, at 161 Second Avenue.

McSherry, Lucy, age 2; of 161 Second Avenue. Daughter of Mary Jane, and of the late Matthew McSherry. 13 March 1941, at 161 Second Avenue.

McSherry, Margaret, age 3; of 161 Second Avenue. Daughter of Mary Jane, and of the late Matthew McSherry. 13 March 1941, at 161 Second Avenue.

McSherry, Mary, age 14; of 161 Second Avenue. Daughter of Mary Jane, and of the late Matthew McSherry. 13 March 1941, at 161 Second Avenue.

McSherry, Mary Jane, age 40; of 161 Second Avenue. Daughter of the late J. J. and Ellen Douglas; widow of Matthew McSherry. 13 March 1941, at 161 Second Avenue.

McSherry, Matthew, age 16; of 161 Second Avenue. Son of Mary Jane, and of the late Matthew McSherry. 13 March 1941, at 161 Second Avenue.

McSherry, Sheila, age 5; of 161 Second Avenue. Daughter of Mary Jane, and of the late Matthew McSherry. 13 March 1941, at 161 Second Avenue.

Malaugh, Margaret, age 18. Daughter of James Malaugh. 14 March 1941, at 10 Burns Street, Dalmuir.

Malcolm, William, age 5. Son of William Bruce Malcolm and Ellen Malcolm. 13 March 1941, at 161 Second Avenue.

Marks, Peter, age 61; of 61 Whitecrook Street. Husband of Janet Paterson Marks. 14 March 1941, at 61 Whitecrook Street.

Marshall, Archibald Brownlie, age 43. Son of Mary Brownlie Marshall, of 3 Killiegrew Road, Glasgow, and of the late Robert Marshall; husband of Margaret Marshall, of 57 Moodiesburn Street, Glasgow. 15 September 1941, at Beardmore Basin, Dalmuir.

Marshall, Johanna Dobbie, age 72; of 12 Beatty Street, Dalmuir. Wife of Peter Marshall. 13 March 1941, at 12 Beatty Street.

Marshall, Peter, age 78; of 12 Beatty Street, Dalmuir. Husband of Johanna Dobbie Marshall, 13 March 1941, at 12 Beatty Street.

Martin, Thomas, age 37; Constable, War Department. Husband of Annie Martin, of 176 Edgefauld Road, Glasgow. 13 March 1941, at Ordnance Factory, Dalmuir.

(For Middlemiss, Eric see Betty, Eric).

Millar, Elizabeth Hunter, age 62; of 1 The Crescent, Dalmuir. Daughter of William and Jane Lawrie, of Gleniffer View, Thorn, Johnstone; wife of John Millar. 14 March 1941, at 1 The Crescent.

Miller, Archibald James, age 61; 13 March 1941, at 9 Pattison Street.

Miller, Eileen Theresa, age 7. 13 March 1941, at 9 Pattison Street.

MILLER, MARY, age 53. 13 March 1941, at 9 Pattison Street.

MILLER, SHEILA, age 10. 13 March 1941, at 9 Pattison Street.

MORRISON, GEORGE, age 83; of Benbow Hotel, Dalmuir. 13 March 1941, at Benbow Hotel.

MORRISON, HELEN, age 38; of 27 Graham Avenue. Wife of Norman Wilkie Morrison. 13 March 1941, at 27 Graham Avenue.

MORRISON, HELEN, age 10; of 27 Graham Avenue. Daughter of Norman Wilkie Morrison, and of Helen Morrison. 13 March 1941, at 27 Graham Avenue.

MORRISON, JOHN, age 39; of 3 Inchlea Street, Glasgow. Son of the late Angus and Catherine McDonald Morrison, of 30 Lionel Ness, Stornoway; husband of Mary Morrison, 15 September 1941, at Beardmore Basin, Dalmuir.

MORRISON, MARGARET RULEU, age 1; of 27 Graham Avenue. Daughter of Norman Wilkie Morrison, and of Helen Morrison. 13 March 1941, at 27 Graham Avenue.

MORRISON, WILLIAM KANE JEFFREYS, age 9; of 27 Graham Avenue. Son of Norman Wilkie Morrison, and of Helen Morrison. 13 March 1941, at 27 Graham Avenue.

MULHERN, GRACE, age 59; of 431 Glasgow Road. 13 March 1941, at 431 Glasgow Road.

MULLINGER, REBECCA, age 50. 13 March 1941, at 72 Second Avenue.

MULLINGER, WILLIAM, age 17. Son of Rebecca Mullinger. 13 March 1941, at 72 Second Avenue.

NISBET, ANNIE, age 45; of 161 Second Avenue. Daughter of John and Martha Cunningham, of Glenruther Terrace, Dalmuir; wife of James Nisbet. 13 March 1941, at 161 Second Avenue.

NISBET, JAMES, age 50; of 161 Second Avenue. Son of Alexander Reid Nisbet, and Christina Reid Nisbet, of 22 Napier Place, Bainsford, Falkirk; husband of Annie Nisbet. 13 March 1941, at 161 Second Avenue.

NISBET, JAMES, age 16; of 161 Second Avenue. Son of James and Annie Nisbet. 13 March 1941, at 161 Second Avenue.

NISBET, JOHN, age 13; of 161 Second Avenue. Son of James and Annie Nisbet. 13 March 1941, at 161 Second Avenue.

PARKE, HELEN, age 19 months; of 19 Gordon Street. Daughter of Samuel and Helen Parke. 13 March 1941, at 19 Gordon Street.

PATTERSON, ANDREW, age 58. 13 March 1941, at 159 Second Avenue.

PEDDIE, SUSANNA, age 74; 14 March 1941, at 57 Whitecrook Street.

PEDEN, ELIZABETH, age 16; of 10 Broom Drive, North Kilbowie. Daughter of Robert and Elizabeth Scott Peden. 13 March 1941, at 10 Broom Drive.

PEDEN, ELIZABETH SCOTT, age 47; of 10 Broom Drive, North Kilbowie. Daughter of the late William and Annie Taylor Scott; wife of Robert Peden. 13 March 1941, at 10 Broom Drive.

PEDEN, ROBERT, age 52; of 10 Broom Drive. North Kilbowie. Son of the late James Dick Peden and Annie Dempster Peden; husband of Elizabeth Scott Peden; 13 March 1941, at 10 Broom Drive.

PEOPLES, JAMES, age 37; of 76 Second Avenue. Son of Margaret Peoples of Church Street, Ramelton, Co. Donegal, Irish Republic, and of the late Charles Peoples; husband of Janet Turpie Gardiner Peoples. 13 March 1941, at 76 Second Avenue.

PEOPLES, JAMES, age 1; of 76 Second Avenue. Son of James and Janet Turpie Gardiner Peoples. 13 March 1941, at 76 Second Avenue.

PEOPLES, JANET TURPIE GARDINER, age 28; of 76 Second Avenue. Daughter of the late John and Janet Turpie Gardiner; wife of James Peoples. 13 March 1941, at 76 Second Avenue.

PILLAR, SAMUEL, age 52; Air Raid Warden; of 14 Beatty Street, Dalmuir. Husband of Mary W. Pillar. 13 March 1941, at 14 Beatty Street.

PORTER, GEORGE, age 56; of 12 Pattison Street, Dalmuir. 13 March 1941, at 12 Pattison Street.

PORTER, SAMUEL, age 63; of 12 Pattison Street, Dalmuir. 13 March 1941, at 12 Pattison Street.

QUIGG, ELIZABETH MCINTOSH, age 18; of 781 Dumbarton Road, Dalmuir. Daughter of H. C. and Mary Niven Quigg. 14 March 1941, at 781 Dumbarton Road.

RAMAGE, SAMUEL DOUGLAS, age 31; Firewatcher; of 56 Boquhanran Road. Son of Elizabeth Bond Ramage, and of the late Robert Robertson Ramage. 13 March 1941, at 76 Second Avenue.

RANKIN, MARGARET BOOMER, age 6. Daughter of David Rankin. 13 March 1941, at 78 Second Avenue.

REAVEY, CHARLOTTE, age 46; of 59 Whitecrook Street. Wife of D. G. Reavey. 14 March 1941, at 59 Whitecrock Street.

REID, AGNES BARBOUR PATERSON, age 41. Daughter of Margaret King, of 42 Kilnside Road, Paisley; wife of James Edward Reid, of 745 Dumbarton Road, 14 March 1941, at Dumbarton Road.

REID, ALASTAIR JOHN MCKENZIE, age 3 months; of 6 Hawthorn Street. Son of Alexander Laird Reid and Elizabeth Reid. 14 March 1941, at 6 Hawthorn Street.

REID, ANNIE, age 46; of 775 Dumbarton Road, Dalmuir. Daughter of the late Thomas and Marion MacNab Sloss; wife of William J. Reid. 14 March 1941, at 775 Dumbarton Road.

REID, RACHEL, age 70. 13 March 1941, at 80 Second Avenue.

RICHMOND, CATHERINE, age 43. Wife of John Richmond. 14 March 1941, at 60 Radnor Street.

RICHMOND, CATHERINE, age 5. Daughter of John and Catherine Richmond. 14 March 1941, at 60 Radnor Street.

RICHMOND, CHRISTINA, age 17. Daughter of John and Catherine Richmond. 14 March 1941, at 60 Radnor Street.

RICHMOND, DOUGLAS, age 10. Son of John and Catherine Richmond. 14 March 1941, at 60 Radnor Street.

RICHMOND, ELIZABETH, age 7. Daughter of John and Catherine Richmond. 14 March 1941, at 60 Radnor Street.

RICHMOND, JANET, age 3. Daughter of John and Catherine Richmond. 14 March 1941, at 60 Radnor Street.

RICHMOND, JOHN, age 41. Husband of Catherine Richmond. 14 March 1941, at 60 Radnor Street.

RICHMOND, JOHN, age 15. Son of John and Catherine Richmond. 14 March 1941, at 60 Radnor Street.

RICHMOND, MARGARET, age 13. Daughter of John and Catherine Richmond. 14 March 1941, at 60 Radnor Street.

ROBERTS, TREVOR PARRY, age 39; of 21 Glasgow Road. 14 March 1941, at 3 Browns Buildings.

ROBERTSON, ANNIE WILSON, age 10; of 64 Crown Avenue. Daughter of Andrew Robertson, and of Margaret McCole Robertson. 14 March 1941, at 64 Crown Avenue.

ROBERTSON, DAVID, age 15; of 64 Crown Avenue. Son of Andrew Robertson, and of Margaret McCole Robertson. 14 March 1941, at 64 Crown Avenue.

ROBERTSON, HENRY, age 49; of 39 Graham Avenue. Husband of Sarah Robertson. 13 March 1941, at Diesel Works.

ROBERTSON, MARGARET, McCOLE, age 46; of 64 Crown Avenue. Wife of Andrew Robertson. 14 March 1941, at 64 Crown Avenue.

ROBERTSON, MARY MCALLISTER, age 12; of 64 Crown Avenue. Daughter of Andrew Robertson, and of Margaret McCole Robertson. 14 March 1941, at 64 Crown Avenue.

ROCKS, ANN, age 1; of 78 Jellicoe Street, Dalmuir. Daughter of Patrick Rocks (Jnr.) and Elizabeth Rocks. 13 March 1941, at 78 Jellicoe Street.

ROCKS, ANNIE, age 54; of 78 Jellicoe Street, Dalmuir. Daughter of Mary Boyle; wife of Patrick Rocks (Senr.), 13 March 1941, at 78 Jellicoe Street.

ROCKS, ELIZABETH, age 28; of 78 Jellicoe Street, Dalmuir. Daughter of Mr. and Mrs. Carruth, of John Knox Street; wife of Patrick Rocks (Junr.), 13 March 1941, at 78 Jellicoe Street.

ROCKS, FRANCIS, age 21; of 78 Jellicoe Street, Dalmuir. Son of Patrick Rocks (Senr.), and of Annie Rocks. 13 March 1941, at 78 Jellicoe Street.

ROCKS, JAMES, age 32; of 78 Jellicoe Street, Dalmuir. Son of Patrick Rocks (Senr.) and of Annie Rocks. 13 March 1941, at 78 Jellicoe Street.

ROCKS, JAMES, age 4; of 78 Jellicoe Street, Dalmuir. Son of Patrick Rocks (Junr.), and of Elizabeth Rocks. 13 March 1941, at 78 Jellicoe Street.

ROCKS, JOHN, age 19; of 78 Jellicoe Street, Dalmuir. Son of Patrick Rocks (Senr.), and of Annie Rocks. 13 March 1941, at 78 Jellicoe Street.

ROCKS, JOSEPH, age 17; of 78 Jellicoe Street, Dalmuir. Son of Patrick Rocks (Senr.), and of Annie Rocks. 13 March 1941, at 78 Jellicoe Street.

ROCKS, MARGARET, age 2; of 78 Jellicoe Street, Dalmuir. Daughter of Patrick Rocks (Junr.) and of Elizabeth Rocks. 13 March 1941, at 78 Jellicoe Street.

ROCKS, PATRICK, age 28; Royal Humane Society Testimonial for Life Saving; of 78 Jellicoe Street, Dalmuir. Son of Patrick Rocks, and of Annie Rocks; husband of Elizabeth Rocks. 13 March 1941, at 78 Jellicoe Street.

ROCKS, PATRICK, age 6; of 78 Jellicoe Street, Dalmuir. Son of Patrick Rocks (Junr.) and Elizabeth Rocks. 13 March 1941, at 78 Jellicoe Street.

ROCKS, THERESA, age 25; of 78 Jellicoe Street, Dalmuir. Daughter of Patrick Rocks (Senr.) and of Annie Rocks. 13 March 1941, at 78 Jellicoe Street.

ROCKS, THOMAS, age 13; of 78 Jellicoe Street, Dalmuir. Son of Patrick Rocks (Senr.), and of Annie Rocks. 13 March 1941, at 78 Jellicoe Street.

ROCKS, THOMAS, age 5 months; of 78 Jellicoe Street, Dalmuir. Son of Patrick Rocks (Junr.), and Elizabeth Rocks. 13 March 1941, at 78 Jellicoe Street.

RUSSELL, IAN MCGREGOR, age 9; of 12 Beatty Street, Dalmuir. Son of Margaret Brown Russell, and of the late John Seward Russell. 14 March 1941, at 12 Beatty Street.

RUSSELL, MARGARET BROWN, age 43; of 12 Beatty Street, Dalmuir. Daughter of Peter and Johanna Dobbie Marshall; widow of John Seward Russell. 13 March 1941, at 12 Beatty Street.

RUSSELL, PETER, age 38. Son of the late Peter and Elizabeth Stewart Russell; husband of Elizabeth Downie Russell, of 6 Stewart Place, Catrine, Mauchline, Ayr. 14 March 1941, at 60 Radnor Street.

SCOTT, ELIZABETH, age 43; of 9 Pattison Street, Dalmuir. Wife of Walter Scott. 13 March 1941, at 9 Pattison Street.

SCOTT, MORAG, age 12; of 9 Pattison Street, Dalmuir. Daughter of Walter Scott, and of Elizabeth Scott. 13 March 1941, at 9 Pattison Street.

SCOTT, NATHANIEL, age 29; of 9 Pattison Street, Dalmuir. Son of Margaret Cravagan Scott. 14 March 1941, at 2 Castle Street.

SCOTT, WALTER, age 7; of 9 Pattison Street, Dalmuir. Son of Walter Scott, and of Elizabeth Scott. 13 March 1941, at 9 Pattison Street.

SCRIMSHIRE, EMMA, age 16; of 128 Second Avenue, Radnor Park. Daughter of Mr. and Mrs. James Scrimshire. 13 March 1941, at Spencer Street.

SEMPLE, SHEILA, age 7; of 104 Canberra Avenue, Dalmuir. Daughter of William and Maria Semple. 14 March 1941, at Burn Street shelter.

(*For* SEMPLE, KATHLEEN, *see Stirling list.*)

SHARP, JEANIE MUNRO, age 48; of 59 Whitecrook Street. 14 March 1941, at 59 Whitecrook Street.

SHAW, ANDREW, age 29. Husband of Jean Shaw, of 10 Elvan Street, Shettleston, Glasgow. 13 March 1941, at Beardmore's Works.

SHAW, ISABELLA SCOTLAND, age 20; of 55 Crown Avenue. Daughter of Adam Shaw. 13 March 1941, at Church Street.

SHUTER, WILLIAM, age 31; of 196 High Street. Dumbarton. Son of Mr. and Mrs. Thomas Shuter. 13 March 1941, at Second Terrace.

SKINNER, ELIZABETH, age 9; of 64 Crown Avenue. Daughter of Robert and Joan Skinner. 14 March 1941, at 64 Crown Avenue.

SKINNER, JOAN, age 43; of 64 Crown Avenue. Daughter of the late John Duncan; wife of Robert Skinner. 14 March 1941, at 64 Crown Avenue.

SKINNER, JOAN ROBERTA, age 4; of 64 Crown Avenue. Daughter of Robert and Joan Skinner. 14 March 1941, at 64 Crown Avenue.

SKINNER, MARGARET JANE, age 12; of 64 Crown Avenue. Daughter of Robert and Joan Skinner. 14 March 1941, at 64 Crown Avenue.

SKINNER, ROBERT, age 10; of 64 Crown Avenue. Son of Robert and Elizabeth Skinner, of 24 Richmond Street; husband of Joan Skinner. 14 March 1941, at 64 Crown Avenue.

SKINNER, ROBERT, age 2; of 64 Crown Avenue. Son of Robert and Joan Skinner. 14 March 1941, at 64 Crown Avenue.

SLATER, JANET SHARP FINDLAY, age 16; daughter of Alexander and Amelia Findlay Slater, of 48 Second Avenue. 13 March 1941, at Spencer Street.

SMART, DAVID, age 11; of 7 Beardmore Street, Dalmuir. Son of James Smart, and of Susan Smart. 14 March 1941, at 7 Beardmore Street.

SMART, ROBERT, age 13 months; of 7 Beardmore Street, Dalmuir. Son of James Smart, and of Susan Smart. 14 March 1941, at 7 Beardmore Street.

SMART, SUSAN, age 36; of 7 Beardmore Street, Dalmuir. Wife of James Smart. 14 March 1941, at 7 Beardmore Street.

SPENCE, JOHN COLQUHOUN, age 58; of 4 Whin Street, North Kilbowie. Husband of Jane Spence. 13 March 1941, at 4 Whin Street.

STEVENS, CECIL, age 41; of 159 Second Avenue. Son of Frederick and Katherina Flynn Stevens, of Cape Town, South Africa; husband of Christina Stevens. 13 March 1941, at 159 Second Avenue.

STEVENS, JAMES, age 77. 13 March 1941, at 74 Second Avenue.

STEVENSON, MARY, age 66; of 6 Second Avenue. Daughter of Sam McKee, of Dromore, Co. Down, Northern Ireland; widow of Daniel Stevenson. 15 March 1941, at 78 Clarence Street.

STEWART, ELIZABETH, age 10; of 9 Pattison Street, Dalmuir. Daughter of Mr. and Mrs. John Stewart. 13 March 1941, at 7 Beardmore Street.

STRACHAN, JANE, age 73; of 9 Pattison Street, Dalmuir. Widow of James Strachan. 13 March 1941, at 9 Pattison Street.

STRUTHERS, JOSEPH, age 37; of 9 Birch Road, Parkhall, Dalmuir. Husband of Elizabeth M. Struthers. 14 March 1941, at 9 Birch Road.

TAYLOR, JAMES, age 17; of 5 Hornbeam Drive, Parkhall, Dalmuir. Son of Mary Taylor. 13 March 1941, at 5 Hornbeam Drive.

THOM, MARGARET, age 71; of 89 Glenburn, Prestwick, Ayr. Widow of Archibald Thom. 13 March 1941, at 9 Pattison Street.

THOMAS, ROSEMARY RUSSELL, age 9; of 170 Hope Street, Glasgow. Daughter of Elsie K. Thomas, and of Russell Llewellyn Thomas. 13 March 1941, at 4 Greer Quad.

THOMAS, RUSSELL LLEWELLYN, age 37; Air Raid Warden; of 170 Hope Street, Glasgow. Husband of Elsie K. Thomas. 13 March 1941, at 4 Greer Quad.

THOMSON, CHRISTINA WILSON, age 19; of 27 Graham Avenue. Daughter of William Thomson, and of Margaret Thomson. 13 March 1941, at 27 Graham Avenue.

THOMSON, MARGARET, age 42; of 27 Graham Avenue. Wife of William Thomson. 13 March 1941, at 27 Graham Avenue.

THOMSON, MARGARET, age 20; of 27 Graham Avenue. Daughter of William Thomson, and of Margaret Thomson. 13 March 1941, at 27 Graham Avenue.

THOMSON, WILLIAMINA, age 24; of 27 Graham Avenue. Daughter of William Thomson, and of Margaret Thomson. 13 March 1941, at 27 Graham Avenue.

(*For* THOMSON, WILLIAM, *see* GEDDES, WILLIAM)

TOLAND, JOHN, age 53; of 6 Cherry Crescent. 13 April 1941, at Trades Hotel, Miller Street.

VENTILLA, HELEN, age 21; of 8 Napier Street. Daughter of Owen and Catherine McParland; wife of Anthony Ventilla. 13 March 1941, at 8 Napier Street.

VENTILLA, LOUIS, age 5; of 4 Napier Street. Son of Michael and Angelina Ventilla. 13 March 1941, at 4 Napier Street.

VENTILLA, MICHAEL, age 64; Italian National; of 4 Napier Street. Husband of Angelina Ventilla. 13 March 1941, at 4 Napier Street.

WADE, JESSIE CHALMERS, age 13; daughter of Robert Currie Low Wade and Helen Wade, of 51 Whitecrook Street. 14 March 1941, at 57 Whitecrook Street. (Her brother William Thomson (or Geddes) was also killed in the same incident.)

WAITE, CHARLES EDWARD, age 34; of 57 Whitecrook Street. Son of Henry and Elizabeth Waite. 14 March 1941, at 57 Whitecrook Street.

WALKER, ANNIE JAMIESON, age 45. Daughter of John and Janet Henderson Brown, of 2 Dalnottar Terrace. Old Kilpatrick, Dumbartonshire; wife of David A. Walker, of 21 Aberconway Street. 14 March 1941, at 59 Whitecrook Street.

WALKER, ARCHIBALD. Son of John Walker, of 10 Buchanan Street. 15 March 1941, at Clydebank.

WALSH, CATHERINE, age 5 weeks; of 1 Second Terrace. Daughter of Ellen Walsh. 13 March 1941, at Janetta Street.

WARK, ROBERT, age 27; of 781 Dumbarton Road, Dalmuir. Son of Jessie Wark, of 10 Hill Street, and of the late Robert Wark; husband of Catherine Ferrier Wark. 14 March 1941, at 781 Dumbarton Road.

WATSON, GEORGE, age 72. Husband of Isabella Watson. 13 March 1941, at 78 Jellicoe Street.

WATSON, GEORGE LOGAN, age 38. Son of George and Isabella Watson. 13 March 1941, at 78 Jellicoe Street.

WATSON, ISABELLA, age 66. Wife of George Watson. 13 March 1941, 78 Jellicoe Street.

WATSON, JAMES, age 36. Son of George and Isabella Watson. 13 March 1941, at 78 Jellicoe Street.

WATSON, LILIAN, age 19. Daughter of George and Isabella Watson. 13 March 1941, at 78 Jellicoe Street.

WESTBURY, ALFRED, age 54; of 2 Castle Street, Dalmuir. Husband of Elizabeth McInnes Westbury. 14 March 1941, at 2 Castle Street.

WESTBURY, ALFRED, age 22; of 2 Castle Street, Dalmuir. Son of Alfred and Elizabeth McInnes Westbury. 14 March 1941, at 2 Castle Street.

WESTBURY, ELIZABETH MCINNES, age 56; of 2 Castle Street, Dalmuir. Wife of Alfred Westbury. 14 March 1941, at 2 Castle Street.

WESTBURY, SAMUEL ALFRED, age 27; of 2 Castle Street, Dalmuir. Son of Alfred and Elizabeth McInnes Westbury. 14 March 1941, at 2 Castle Street.

WESTBURY, WALTER, age 13; of 2 Castle Street, Dalmuir. Son of Alfred and Elizabeth McInnes Westbury. 14 March 1941, at 2 Castle Street.

WHITE, ROBERT, age 18; of 48 Crown Avenue. Son of John and Jane White. 13 March 1941, at La Scala Picture House.

WILLIAMS, JESSIE ANNIE, age 74; of 431 Glasgow Road. 13 March 1941, at 2 Napier Street.

WILLIAMSON, ANNIE, age 5. Daughter of Gnr. R. Williamson, R.A. and of Catherine Williamson. 13 March 1941, at 74 Second Avenue.

WILLIAMSON, CATHERINE, age 37. Wife of Gnr. R. Williamson, R.A. 13 March 1941, at 74 Second Avenue.

WILLIAMSON, JAMES, age 7. Son of Gnr. R. Williamson, R.A., and of Catherine Williamson. 13 March 1941, at 74 Second Avenue.

WILLIAMSON, JANETTA, age 6. Daughter of Gnr. R. Williamson, R.A., and of Catherine Williamson. 13 March 1941, at 74 Second Avenue.

WILSON, ARCHIBALD, age 31; of 42 Millbrix Avenue, Glasgow. Son of Janet York Wilson, and of the late Archibald Wilson. 14 March 1941, at 60 Radnor Street.

WILSON, DAVID, age 29. Son of Mr. and Mrs. John Wilson, of 342 Nuneaton Street, Glasgow. 13 March 1941, at 76 Second Avenue.

WOOD, HUGH, age 36; of 14 First Terrace. Husband of Margaret Wood. 13 March 1941, at Wardens' Post, Janetta Street.

WOOD, JOHN, age 15; of 14 First Terrace. Son of Margaret Wood, and of Hugh Wood. 13 March 1941, at Wardens' Post, Janetta Street.

WOOD, MARGARET, age 5; of 14 First Terrace. Daughter of Margaret Wood, and of Hugh Wood. 13 March 1941, at Wardens' Post, Janetta Street.

WOODS, JAMES, age 9; of 159 Second Avenue. Son of Daniel Woods. 13 March 1941, at Second Avenue.

WRIGHT, CHRISTINA, age 26; of 78 Clarence Street. Daughter of Dougald and Maria Wright. 15 March 1941, at 78 Clarence Street.

WRIGHT, DOUGALD, age 53; of 78 Clarence Street. Son of Christina Wright; husband of Maria Wright. 15 March 1941, at 78 Clarence Street.

WRIGHT, MARIA, age 55; of 78 Clarence Street. Daughter of Sam McKee, of Dromore, Co. Down, Northern Ireland; wife of Dougald Wright. 15 March 1941, at 78 Clarence Street.

WRIGHT, MARTHA, age 31; of 78 Clarence Street. Daughter of Dougald and Maria Wright. 15 March 1941, at 78 Clarence Street.

YOUNG, MARIE, age 6; of 7 Spencer Street. 13 March 1941, at 1 Spencer Street.

APPENDIX B

NOTABLE NIGHT ATTACKS ON U.K. CITIES,
November, 1940—May, 1941
(Statistics compiled from German sources)

1940	Place	No. of Aircraft	Tons of High Explosive	Incendiary Containers
Nov. 14	Coventry	449	503	881
15	London	358	414	1,142
19	Birmingham	357	403	810
20	,,	116	132	296
22	,,	204	227	457
28	Liverpool-Birkenhead	324	356	860
29	London	335	380	820
Dec. 8	,,	413	387	3,188
11	Birmingham	278	277	685
12	Sheffield	336	355	457
20	Liverpool-Birkenhead	205	205	761
21	,,	299	280	940
22	Manchester	270	272	1,032
23	,,	171	195	893
29	London	136	127	613
1941				
Jan. 3	Bristol	178	154	1,488
Mar. 10	Portsmouth	238	193	1,291
12	Liverpool-Birkenhead	316	303	1,782
13	Glasgow-Clydeside	236	272	1,650
14	,,	203	231	782
18	Hull	378	316	2,140
19	London	479	467	3,397
Apr. 7	Glasgow-Clydeside	179	204	722
8	Coventry	237	315	1,183
9	Birmingham	237	285	1,110
10	,,	206	246	1,183
May 3	Liverpool-Birkenhead	298	363	1,386
4	Belfast	204	237	2,667
5	Glasgow-Clydeside	386	351	1,300
6	,,	232	271	1,140
10	London	507	711	2,393

Note: The dates refer to the commencement of the raids.
(The above table has been extracted from Basil Collier: *The Defence of the United Kingdom* (1957) by permission of H.M. Stationery Office.)

APPENDIX C

LUFTWAFFE, THIRD AIR FLEET, WEST FRANCE
PLAN OF ATTACK ON GLASGOW AND CLYDESIDE,
March 13-14, 1941
(Statistics from German sources)

Time	Unit	Type	No.	Altitude (in metres)
9.34–9.50	I. K.G. 27	He 111	4	2,500–4,000
9.40–10.05	I. K.G. 54	Ju 88	12	2,500–4,000
9.54–10.25	K. Gr. 100	He 111	12	2,000–3,600
10.05–10.22	I. K.G. 27	He 111	9	3,200–4,000
10.13–10.25	II. K.G. 27	He 111	5	3,000–3,500
10.27–11.30	I. K.G. 1	He 111	12	1,900–3,200
10.47–11.40	II. K.G. 55	He 111	9	Below 3,000
10.50–11.14	III. K.G. 1	Ju 88	7	2,400–3,300
10.55–2.54	K.G. 77	Ju 88	28	3,000–3,200
11.30–11.55	III. K.G. 26	He 111	12	2,800–3,400
2.24–3.10	II. K.G. 76	Ju 88	16	2,800–3,400
2.50	III. K.G. 1	Ju 88	4	3,000–3,500

Abbreviations: He—Heinkel; Ju—Junkers; K.G.—Kampfgeschwader (Bomber Squadron); K. Gr.—Kampfgruppe (Bomber group).

APPENDIX D

LUFTWAFFE, THIRD AIR FLEET, WEST FRANCE ATTACK ON GLASGOW AND CLYDESIDE, March, 14-15, 1941
(Statistics from German sources)

Time	Unit	Type	No.	Altitude (metres)	Bombs and Targets
9.30–10.15	I. K.G. 27	He 111	7	2,500–3,200	14 250k; 7 500k; 2,016 IB —target unspecified
9.45–9.55	III. K.G. 51	Ju 88	3	1,600–3,600	3 250k; 3 500k—east of river; harbour area
9.45–10.30	II. K.G. 76	Ju 88	14	1,500–3,500	140 50k; 56 250k; 3 500k —oil tanks
10.05–10.45	II. K.G. 27	He 111	13	3,000–4,000	North-west sector of target area 'a'—oil depot
10.07–10.35	I. K.G. 27	He 111	6	2,000–3,900	6 250k; 4 250k (DA); 6 500k—target unspecified
10.08	I. K.G. 51	Ju 88	1	3,000	1 250k; 1 500k (DA)— Rolls-Royce Works, Hillington
10.14	II. K.G. 51	Ju 88	1	3,200	1 250k; 1 500k—Rolls-Royce Works, Hillington
10.15–10.46	K.G. 77	Ju 88	10	3,000–3,300	20 50k; 22 250k; 6 250k (DA)—target unspecified
10.15–11.00	K. Gr. 100	He 111	7	3,000–3,800	14 250k; 3,024 IB—target I
10.20–11.33	III. K.G. 1	Ju 88	6	3,000–3,500	20 250k; 3 250k (DA); 1 500k—target area 'b'
10.23–11.40	I. K.G. 1	He 111	12	2,500–3,500	4 50k; 1 500k; 13,104 IB— target unspecified
10.30–11.10	I. K.G. 55	He 111	9	2,000–2,500	15 250k; 8 500k; 2,160 IB —Rolls-Royce Works, Hillington; Princes' and Kingston Docks
10.40–11.10	II. K.G. 55	He 111	8	2,000–3,000	24 250k; 9 500k; 576 IB— target unspecified
10.50–11.05	K. Gr. 806	He 111	10	2,000–3,500	40 250k—Rolls-Royce Works, Hillington
11.21–01.50	III. K.G. 26	He 111	5	3,100–3,500	5 500k; 2,880 IB—target unspecified

Abbreviations: DA—delayed action; He—Heinkel; IB—incendiary bomb; Ju— Junkers; k—kilogram; K.G.—Kampfgeschwader (Bomber squadron); K. Gr.— Kampfgruppe (Bomber group).

The aircraft listed above (112 out of 132 which left France) were the major portion of the total number, 203, engaged in the raid on Clydeside. Two of the units mentioned,

K. Gr. 100 and III. K.G. 26, were normally used as pathfinder forces. If the numbers of bombs dropped by aircraft of the Third Air Fleet—232 50 kilo, 252 250 kilo, 15 250 kilo (delayed action), 44 500 kilo, 1 500 kilo (delayed action), 1 1,000 kilo, 25,488 incendiary —are compared with the totals for the whole raid given in the Luftwaffe Headquarters report—222 50 kilo, 249 250 kilo, 15 250 kilo (delayed action), 42 500 kilo, 3 1,000 kilo, 781 incendiary containers, 54 parachute mines, 92 oil bombs—it is obvious that there are some discrepancies. Both reports are dated May 15, 1941.

EFFECT OF RAIDS OF MARCH, 13-15, 1941, ON INDUSTRIAL CONCERNS

(From report of Glasgow Emergency Reconstruction Panel, April 1, 1941)

Firm	What Making	Damage	State of Production April 1, 1941
Aitchison Blair Ltd.	Small marine engines	Building partly wrecked; machine tools damaged	No production for several days; first production in 2 months
Arnott Young & Co., Ltd.	Metal stores	—	Normal
Beardmore's (Diesel) Ltd.	Heavy armcur plate. Heat treatment of heavy guns	2/3 of main shop wrecked. 2 furnaces hit by H.E. bombs. All furnaces stopped	9 furnaces in operation. Production normal by mid-April
Brockhouse & Co. Ltd.	Automobile parts	Blast damage to roof and walls	Normal
John Brown & Co., Ltd.	Shipbuilding	2 timber stores and pattern store destroyed. Experiment tank, funnel shed and shafting shop badly damaged. Roofs of brass finishing shop, tool room and pattern store damaged	Normal in shipyard and machine shops; almost normal elsewhere
Clyde Blowers Ltd.	Boiler equipment	Severe blast damage to roofs and walls	Normal
Dawson & Downie, Ltd.	Marine pumps	Fairly severe blast damage to roofs and walls	Almost normal
Royal Ordnance Factory, Dal-	Ordnance	Severe damage to roofs of factory. Offices damaged	Returning to normal production
Singer's Manufacturing Co., Ltd.	Armaments; sewing machines	Timber yard, sawmill, wood preparing dept., small electric motors dept. with stock, maintenance dept. with stock, counting house, shipping shed with contents all destroyed. Foundry, forge, gas-	50% of war production restored; sewing production—nil

producers, locomotive
shed, main offices,
canteen all partly
damaged

Steedman & McAllister	Lifebelts	Blast damage to walls and roofs	Almost normal
Strathclyde Hosiery Co., Ltd.	Hosiery	Building destroyed	No production
Turner's Asbestos Cement Co.	Asbestos sheeting	Blast damage to walls and roofs	Almost normal
D. & J. Tullis, Ltd.	Heavy machine tools	H.E. bomb in machine shop; severe blast damage to walls and roofs. 8 machine tools damaged	70% normal production

APPENDIX F

LIST OF BOMBS DROPPED ON CLYDEBANK,
March 13-15 and May 5-7, 1941

THIS list was compiled from Burgh Surveyor records and the record of unexploded bombs from Civil Defence Controller's reports. Exploded mines in many cases have been recorded as high-explosive bombs, and it is known that at least 8 parachute mine caps were recovered. It was not found possible to separate the bombs dropped in March from those dropped in May, but it is known that out of the total, 14 exploded bombs, 3 unexploded bombs and 2 exploded parachute mines only were dropped on the two nights in May. The locations of bombs are marked on large scale maps prepared in the Burgh Surveyor's office; photocopies of the maps are kept in Clydebank Public Library.

No.	Location	Type
1–5	North of Auchentoshan Distillery	X HE
6–10	North-east of Auchentoshan Distillery	,,
11, 12	Mount Blow grounds	,,
13	Recreation grounds	,,
14–16	East of Auchentoshan Distillery	,,
17–20	East of Auchentoshan Lodge	,,
21–23	South-east of Auchentoshan House	,,
24, 25	At Mount Blow Lodge	,,
26	North-west of Mount Blow Lodge	,,
27–30	North-west of Auchentoshan House	,,
31	North of Auchentoshan House	,,
32, 33	East of Auchentoshan House	,,
34–38	South of Auchentoshan House	,,
39	South-east of Auchentoshan House	,,
40, 41	South-west of Auchentoshan House	,,
42, 43	Ocean Field	,,
44–47	Boulevard, south of Old Street	,,
48–51	North of Parkhall Terrace	,,
52–54	North of Manse	,,
55–57	West of Manse	,,
58–60	South-west of Manse	,,
61	Rear of house in Maple Drive	,,
62	Boulevard, south of nursery	,,
63	In roadway at Birch Road	,,
64	Chestnut Drive	,,
65	Rear of Maple Drive	,,
66	Beech Drive	,,
67	Rear of house in Beech Drive	,,
68–70	Near railway at Canberra Avenue	,,
71	Freelands Place junction	,,
72–74	Dumbarton Road near Delhi Avenue	,,
75	Canal near Delhi Avenue	,,

No.	Location	Type
76–79	Mount Blow grounds	X HE
80, 81	Running track, Mount Blow	,,
82	Mount Blow grounds	,,
83	Pine Road	,,
84	Cedar Avenue	,,
85	Dumbarton Road near Auckland Street	,,
86	Auckland Street	,,
87	East of Mount Blow Road	,,
88–90	Lilac Avenue	,,
91	Near Duntocher Burn	,,
92–95	Public Park, Parkhall	,,
96–119	Parkhall golf course	,,
120	West of Dunclutha House	,,
121–125	Near Golf View, Parkhall	,,
126, 127	Allotments south of Golf View	,,
128, 129	Overtoun Road	,,
130	Near tennis courts	,,
131	Junction of Risk Street and Duntocher Road	,,
132	Ash Road	,,
133	Elm Road	,,
134	Beech Drive	,,
135	Planetree Road	,,
136, 137	Hornbeam Drive	,,
138–140	Sycamore Drive	,,
141, 142	Rowan Drive	,,
143, 144	Limetree Drive	,,
145	Near Poplar Drive	,,
146	Junction of Poplar Drive and Duntocher Road	,,
147–154	In grounds of Parkhall	,,
155	Parkhall golf course	,,
156, 157	Near Braemar House	,,
158	Rear of Poplar Drive	,,
159, 160	Near junction of Birch Road and Hornbeam Road	,,
161	Near junction of Birch Road and Limetree Road	,,
162, 163	Duntocher Road near school	,,
164	North of Duntocher Road and Boquhanran Park	,,
165	Boquhanran Park	,,
166–169	North of school	,,
170	Parkhall Park, west side	,,
171	Parkhall Park, south side	,,
172	Railway near Swindon Street	,,
173	Rear of Swindon Street	,,
174	Rear of Beardmore Street	,,
175	Church Hall, Roberts Street	,,
176	Roberts Street	,,
177	Dumbarton Road near Roberts Street	,,
178	Junction of Dumbarton Road and Dunn Street	,,
179	West of Dunn Street	,,

No.	Location	Type
180	Pattison Street	X HE
181–183	Junction of Dumbarton Road and Burns Street	,,
184	Junction of Dumbarton Road and Castle Street	,,
185, 186	Castle Square	,,
187, 188	Junction of Castle Street and Jellicoe Street	,,
189, 190	Near Beatty Street	,,
191, 192	Junction of Scott Street and Dumbarton Road	,,
193	Near Burns Street	,,
194	Junction of Duntocher Road and Risk Street	,,
195	North of Brook Street	,,
196	Between Park Road and Brook Street	,,
197, 198	Park Road at allotments	,,
199	St. Stephen's R.C. Church	,,
200, 201	Railway at Park Road	,,
201a	Ramsay Street	,,
202	Railway at Park Road	,,
203	Timber yard at Dalmuir	,,
204	Railway, Singer Road	,,
205, 206	Railway, South View	,,
207	Near Bowling Green, South View	,,
208–210	Near junction of Stevenson Street and Duntocher Road	,,
211	Duntocher Road near Regent Street	,,
212	Junction of Overtoun Road and Duntocher Road	,,
213, 214	Near Regent Street	,,
215, 216	Parkhall Park	,,
217	South of Methven Street	,,
218	Junction of Dumbarton Road and Duntocher Road	,,
219, 220	North and south ends of Ferguson Street	,,
221	East of Ramsay Street	,,
222	North of Albert Road	,,
223–225	Near school, Albert Road	,,
226–227	Second Avenue	,,
228	Junction of Boquhanran Road and Albert Road	,,
229–232	Singer's Recreation Ground	,,
233	Singer's Timber Yard	,,
234	Singer's Sports Ground	,,
235	Janetta Street School	,,
236, 237	Junction of Janetta Street and West Thomson Street	,,
238, 239	Boquhanran School	,,
240	Junction of Church Street and Circular Road	,,
241	Rear of Crown Avenue	,,
242	Junction of Third and Second Terraces	,,
243	Rear of First Terrace	,,
244	Green Street	,,
245	Tennis Courts, Singer's	,,
246	,, ,, ,,	UX HE

No.	Location	Type
247	Junction of Great Western Road and Kilbowie Road	X HE
248	Junction of Duntocher Road and Kilbowie Road	,,
249	Boulevard, near Kilbowie Road	,,
250–253	North of Williamson Street	,,
254, 255	Briar Drive	,,
256–258	North of Whin Street	,,
259, 260	South of Whin Street	,,
261–265	North-east of Williamson Street	,,
266–268	Field north-east of Boulevard	,,
269	Rear of Greer Quadrant	,,
270	West Thomson Street	,,
271	South of West Thomson Street	,,
272	Rear of Cornock Crescent	,,
273	Cornock Crescent	,,
274	Junction of Kilbowie Road and Radnor Street	,,
275, 276	Junction of Singer Street and Radnor Street	,,
277	Junction of Singer Street and Graham Avenue	,,
278	Allotment Gardens south of Crown Avenue	,,
279	Rear of Crown Avenue	,,
280	Crown Avenue	,,
281	Rear of Crown Avenue (north)	,,
282	Junction of Radnor Street and Granville Street	,,
283	Near Boulevard	,,
284	North of North Kilbowie House	,,
285	Rear of Clarence Street	,,
286	North of Drumry Road	,,
287–289	Sandpit, Boulevard	,,
290	Near sandpit, Boulevard	,,
291	South of Knappers	,,
292	Canal west of Singer's Works	,,
293, 294	Football Ground, Singer's	,,
295	South of Football Ground	,,
296, 297	West of Agamemnon Street	,,
298–299	East of Football Ground. Singer's	,,
300	,, ,, ,, ,, ,,	X PM
301–303	West of Singer's Factory	X HE
304	North-west of Singer's Factory	,,
305, 306	Direct hit, Singer's West Building	,,
307, 308	West of Singer's Offices	,,
309	South of Singer's West Building	X HE
310	Canal south of Singer's Building	,,
311	Railway south of Singer's Works	,,
312	Clydebank Engineering Works	X PM
313, 314	,, ,, ,,	X HE
315	Dumbarton Road at John Brown's	,,
316	North of Graham Avenue	,,
317	Kilbowie Road near Singer's Station	,,

No.	Location	Type
318	South-west of Cinema, Second Avenue	X HE
319	Junction of Second Avenue and Kilbowie Road	,,
320	Kilbowie Road opposite Singer's	X PM
321	Graham Street	X HE
322	Main Building, Singer's	,,
323, 324	Kilbowie Cemetery	,,
325	Near junction of Boulevard and Drumry Road	,,
326–329	North of Kilbowie Railway Station	,,
330	Rear Kilbowie Road near Singer's	,,
331	Rear Livingstone Street	,,
332	Rear Rosebery Place	,,
333	Rear Miller Street	,,
334	Hotel, Millar Street	,,
335	Library, Dumbarton Road	,,
336	Municipal Buildings	,,
337	Bruce Street	,,
338	Junction of Somerville Street and Dumbarton Road	,,
339	Kilbowie Road and Chambers Street	,,
340	North end, Gordon Street	,,
341, 342	Gordon Street	,,
343, 344	Kilbowie Works (Tullis)	,,
345–348	Tenements, Livingstone Street	,,
349	Livingstone Street	,,
350	Victoria Street	,,
351	Whitecrook Lane	,,
352	Junction of Whitecrook Street and Stanford Street	,,
353, 354	Stanford Street	,,
355	Rear of Whitecrook Street	,,
356	Victoria Street	,,
357, 358	Engineering Works, Stanford Street	,,
359	Cochno Street	,,
360	Junction of Cochno Street and Dean Street	,,
361	South of Dean Street	,,
362	Playing fields north of Dean Street	,,
363, 364	North of main railway line	,,
365, 366	Canal bank, east side of town	,,
367	Tenements, Glasgow Road (Hume Street)	,,
368	Junction of Glasgow Road and Canal Street	,,
369, 370	Clydebank Engineering Works	X PM
371, 372	,, ,, ,,	X HE
373	South-east of Rectory, Dunmore Street	,,
374	Rear of John Knox Street	,,
375	Junction of Brown Street and Clyde Street	,,
376	North side of Dean Street	,,
377, 378	Recreation Ground, North Elgin Street	,,
379	Rear of Macdonald Crescent	,,
380	East Barns Street	,,
381	Rear of McGregor Street	,,

No.	Location	Type
382-386	North-east of Sinclair Street	X HE
387	Millburn Avenue	,,
388	Near junction of Glasgow Road and Napier Street	,,
389	Rear of John Knox Street	,,
390	Bowling green, Stevenson Street	UX HE
391-393	Turner's Asbestos Works	,,
394	Rear of 11 Stewart Street	,,
395	107 Duntocher Road	,,
396	50 yards west of car terminus	UX PM
397	Near Golf View	,,
398	Union Manse, Duntocher Road	UX HE
399	Near Royal Ordnance Factory	,,
400, 401	Castle Square	,,
402	Dalmuir Canal Bridge	,,
403	1 Beatty Street	,,
404	Cul-de-sac at Lilac Avenue	,,
405	Public Park, Dalmuir	,,
406	Dalmuir Golf Course, 18th tee	,,
407	20 Alder Road	,,
408	64 Albert Road	,,
409	9 Second Avenue	,,
410	Green Street	,,
411	11 Montrose Street	,,
412	Braidfield Farm	,,
413	Near Duntocher Bridge	,,
414-416	Singer's, West Gate	,,
417	Junction of Boulevard and Drumry Road	UX PM
418	Healthy Burn, Boulevard	UX HE
419	Near Hawthorn Street	,,
420	Cornock Street	,,
421	Junction of Birch Road and Maple Drive	UX PM
422	Kilbowie Cemetery	UX HE
423	Field west of Millburn Avenue	UX PM
424	Opposite Hailing Station	UX HE
425, 426	In water, opposite East Wharf	UX PM
427	Works Department gate, Livingstone Street	UX HE
428	Junction of Stevenson Street and Overtoun Road	,,
429	Park Road at bus halt	,,
430	Tennis courts, Public Park	,,
431	Beardmore's coal pit	,,
432	Risk Street near Park	,,
433	Scott Street	,,
434	Ground west of Boquhanran Road	,,
435	Castle Square	,,
436	South of Mount Blow House	UX PM

No.	Location	Type
437	Between Dunn Street and Swindon Street	UX HE
438	Mount Blow Road	,,
439	Dunedin, Duntocher Road	,,
440	16 Overtoun Road	,,

Abbreviations: HE—high explosive bomb; PM—parachute mine; UX—unexploded; X—exploded.

APPENDIX G

ROLL OF HONOUR

AITKENHEAD, GEORGE, foreman, Clydebank and District Water Trust—King's Commendation.

ANDERSON, JOAN, nurse, Knightswood Emergency Hospital—British Empire Medal.

ATKINSON, JOSEPH, fireman—King's Commendation.

BALLANTYNE, ALEXANDER, Home Guard officer—George Medal.

CAMPBELL, HUGH, ambulance driver—Order of the British Empire.

CAMPBELL, WILLIAMINA, nurse, Glasgow—King's Commendation.

CLOSS, JAMES, party leader, Red Cross—Distinguished Service Certificate.

CRAIG, JAMES, foreman, Rescue Party—George Medal.

FOX, ISAAC, fire fighter, Rutherglen—King's Commendation.

HALDANE, MARY B., ambulance attendant—Order of the British Empire.

HENDRY, CHARLES, police constable—Order of the British Empire.

HERON, ALEXANDER, firemaster—George Medal.

LOGAN, DAVID, foreman, Rescue Party—Order of the British Empire.

MACLEAN, JOHN, fireman—King's Commendation.

MACLEOD, JOHN, police sergeant—George Medal.

MACMARTIN, MORAG, nurse, Dumbarton—King's Commendation.

MCWILLIAM, JAMES, assistant engineer, Clydebank and District Water Trust—British Empire Medal.

MEIKLEJOHN, JAMES, fireman—King's Commendation.

MORRISON, JOHN, assistant firemaster—King's Commendation.

MURPHY, JOHN, member, Red Cross—Distinguished Service Certificate.

SMITH, JOHN, foreman, Rescue Party—Order of the British Empire.

SMYTH, PATRICK, postman, Dalmuir Post Office—British Empire Medal.

STANLEY, MAY, nurse, Knightswood Emergency Hospital—King's Commendation.

STEELE, JOHN S., A.R.P. Deputy Head Warden—Order of the British Empire.

STEWART, JAMES, corporal, Home Guard—British Empire Medal.

STEWART, JOHN, foreman, Rescue Party—George Medal.

THORBURN, DAVID, Head Section Leader, Red Cross—Distinguished Service Certificate.

WEBB, JAMES, fireman—King's Commendation.

APPENDIX H

EXTRACTS FROM SCHOOL LOG OF DUMBARTON ACADEMY, SESSION 1940-41

September 3: The school re-opened today. The grand total of pupils is 658, and of these there are 34 Clydebank pupils in III, 51 in IV, 31 in V, 5 in VI—121.

February 11: Fire watching started in the school with 14 shifts. There are 5 watchers in each shift and the Saturday and Sunday shifts are duplicated. 16 men, 12 women, 48 boys and 4 girls are on duty. Everyone volunteered most readily.

March 3: The Leaving Certificate Examinations commenced today under War Time Regulations.

March 14: Last night there was a serious Air Raid on the Clyde Area. Clydebank suffered badly and transport of pupils and teachers from this part was much interrupted. Many of the senior pupils were on duty all night and many others, pupils and teachers, had no sleep during the night. The S.M.C. ordered the closing of the school for the day.

March 15: On Friday night the Air Raid was continued with equal severity. Very few of the Clydebank pupils, nearly all of whom have been evacuated, have come to school. By 11.30 all the teachers were present. The Leaving Certificate Examinations in Art, Dynamics, Chemistry and Commercial Subjects have been cancelled. 80 windows have been broken in the school but no further damage.

March 19: So far, of the Clydebank pupils the following are accounted for:
VI Girls, 1; VI Boys, 4: V Girls, 5; V Boys, 24; IV Girls, 12; IV Boys, 10; IIIc Girls, 12; IIIc Boys, 2—61.

John MacLeod police sergeant

Hugh Campbell, ambulance driver

David Logan, foreman, Rescue Party

John Smith, foreman, Rescue Party

Mary B. Haldane, ambulance attendant

John Stewart, foreman, Rescue Party

James Craig, foreman, Rescue Party

Charles Hendry, police constable